if you're so brilliant...
HOW COME YOU DON'T HAVE AN E-STRATEGY?

the essential guide to online business

matt haig

series editor: peter cheverton

First published in 2002

Kogan Page Limited
120 Pentonville Road
London N1 9JN
UK

Kogan Page US
22 Broad Street
Milford CT 06460
USA

© Matt Haig, 2002

British Library Cataloguing in Publication Data

A CIP record for this book is available from the British Library.

ISBN 0 7494 3727 8

Typeset by Saxon Graphics Ltd, Derby
Printed and bound in Great Britain by Bell & Bain Ltd, Glasgow

Contents

Series Editor's foreword

Of course, you *are* brilliant, and so will have recognized the point behind the challenging title of this book. This is an issue of high importance and the title is simply an observation that, behind all that brilliance, there's something bothering you, something irritating you, something frustrating you.

The purpose of this *'If You're So Brilliant…'* series is to help you deal with the kind of frustrations that occur across a range of burning business issues. Authors have deliberately targeted the things that are causing the greatest anxiety, right now. As the series develops, the focus will remain on issues that are both topical and of high priority to both the individual and to their business.

Whether it is a continued inability to 'get that marketing plan written', to develop a workable and profitable e-strategy, to build the kind of brand you *really want* and *really should have* or perhaps even simply to understand your accountant, this series is designed to help. The style is deliberately fast and direct and will not dwell too much on theory. Indeed, in such a slim volume it is often necessary to assume certain knowledge and skills beyond the immediate scope of the topic.

So, what frustration makes you pick up this particular title? Perhaps you are already trying to develop a strategy for doing business online, or maybe you are beyond that and are now trying to make it happen, profitably. Whatever your starting point, it's bothering you.

This issue has surely been the cause of more guilt among business people, more stress, more anxiety about falling behind, and more reckless and poorly managed expenditure with frighteningly opportunistic suppliers than any other business issue of our times. The sighs of relief at the failure of dot.com after dot.com could be heard across the country – *'great, now we can drop that damned e-business project'* – but of course, you can't. The bogey hasn't gone away, its just become a whole lot clearer that this isn't an instant panacea for all business ills, but nor is it something that has to turn your business upside down.

What you *can* do is to learn from the experiences of the pioneers, good and bad. You can resolve to plan the development of an e-strategy for your own business, in whatever form it may take, to suit your own circumstances and not to feel you must ape what a hundred pundits said was an easy route to fame and fortune. (The pundits, of course, were urging you on with your money, not theirs.) And most importantly of all you can resolve to do all this with the same care and insistence on an appropriate return as you would for any other significant investment project.

This book will help you with that resolve.

Peter Cheverton
Series Editor

Preface

There are as many different opinions on the commercial value of the Internet as there are businesses. Some believe it can be the answer to all their business prayers while others view the Web as over-hyped and best left alone. Neither view is correct. While an Internet presence can certainly add value to any business, it only works wonders if your business is built on solid ground in the first place. Equally, no matter how strong your business is in the 'real world', it is wrong to presume that the Internet is not able to affect it. The chances are, it already has.

The purpose of this book is to provide you with a sober-headed view of how the Internet can be integrated within your existing operation in order to achieve even better results. It also aims to explain why many Web sites and e-marketing efforts fail to hit the target, while others manage to become online successes. The emphasis throughout is on providing a general overview of the main areas to consider without getting too bogged down in unnecessary technical details. As such, the guide is intended to be concise, practical and to the point.

Getting ready for e-business

Your firm is already an Internet business. No, trust me. It is. The reason I can tell you this with such certainty is because every active business in the UK is now a part of the digital age.

You may not have an e-strategy, you may not even have a Web site, but you will in some way or another be affected by the Internet economy.

Now the dot.com dust has settled, every business must embrace the Internet

Do you use e-mail? Are your competitors increasing their online activity? Are you facing new competition from Internet-based rivals? Are your customers window-shopping on the Web as well as in the real world? Do you search the Web for market information?

If you can answer yes to any of these questions, you are no longer immune to cyberspace and the baffling chaos it may so far have presented you with.

THE NEW BUSINESS DIVIDE

The new business divide is therefore not between Internet businesses and their bricks-and-mortar counterparts, but between businesses that acknowledge the significance of the Internet and those who are ignoring it until it goes away and leaves them alone. The only snag facing businesses in this latter category is the fact that e-business is still here, and, contrary to the negative publicity it has received, it's doing better than ever.

That's right. For all the media hype around the many misguided and ill-fated Internet ventures which have met premature ends over the past few years, more business activity is being conducted via the Web than ever before. The lesson to be learned from the dot.com disasters is not that the Internet doesn't matter, but rather that solid and realistic business plans are still important. Even in today's uncertain economic environment, e-commerce growth remains unfaltering.

What this means is that companies that continue to believe that the Internet is something which happens to other businesses are going to find it increasingly hard to compete. That is not to say that every business should stop what it's doing and transfer its entire operation to the Web. This is a both/and not an either/or situation, which probably explains why many of the most successful e-businesses, such as Tesco.com, have a very strong offline presence.

The challenge lies in being able to seamlessly add an effective online element to your offline business. This clearly signifies different things for different companies. For some, the Web may be a useful sales channel. For others it may prove to be a fruitful marketing tool, or simply a way to communicate information to key audiences (customers, the press, competitors, suppliers, investors, employees etc.).

Although it would be unwise to believe that the Internet can act as some sort of panacea, smoothing out fundamental business problems with ease, it would be equally foolish to underestimate its potential. As Thomas Petzinger put it a few years ago, in his book *The New Pioneers*, 'the Internet explains how a single entrepreneur can create Amazon.com, the world's largest bookstore, on little more than a great idea.' Although the optimistic 'gold rush' mentality evident in that book is no longer wholly appropriate to the new business era we have just entered, there can be little doubt that the Internet can add value to practically every business, of whatever size. Certainly, ignoring the Internet is no longer possible. An e-strategy should therefore no longer be seen as an optional extra, but as an integral part of any business looking to move forward.

As the old scientist's cliché succinctly puts it, the future is already here.

THE INTERNET 'CLICKOCRACY'

Owing to the 'clickocracy' of the Internet, a Web site can set up shop with a miniscule budget and end up competing with the big guns. Indeed, many of the big guns themselves – including MP3.com, CDNow and Yahoo! – were initially set up with very little financial backing. Similarly, many of the sites which have failed to last even through the medium-term launched with megabucks. For instance, the urban clothing retailer Boo.com started with US $125 million and cratered in May 2000, only six months after it launched. So contrary to what some would have us believe, size isn't everything in cyberspace. It's what you do with it that counts.

Although most sites will not have the budget, or the technology, of an Amazon or an eBay, many of the factors which set them apart are as much a result of sticking to core values as their six-figure spending plans. These values can be applied, with success, to sites of practically every scale. However, it would be a mistake for, say, a small independent bookseller to compete with Amazon on its own terms (and not just because Amazon has patented the 'One Click' shopping technology which has made it famous). Owing to the fact that the Web is becoming increasingly crowded with like-minded Web sites, differentiation is essential for long-term survival.

Size isn't everything in cyberspace

As David S Pottruck and Harry Pearce wrote in *Clicks and Mortar*, 'the new economy rewards constant improvement and innovation, and these are derived from the minds and imaginations of people. To compete, we have to innovate faster than the next guy – who is trying to do the same thing. And of course, the next guy is no longer just in the office building across the street or across town, but could be anywhere, in any garage or carriage-house, in just about any country in the world.'

Another way the Internet clickocracy can affect a business is by providing aggrieved customers with a voice.

In cyberspace, the truth is always out there. If the 'truth' undermines the company message then the company is in trouble. The Information Age is also the age of customer feedback. As the highly influential Internet guru Esther Dyson recently told a packed seminar at the London Business

School: 'Things are two-way now. Readers are talking back to newspapers, vendors to buyers and citizens to governments.' If someone has a grudge against a company, they can easily share this grudge with thousands of other similarly disgruntled customers.

The proliferation of 'anti-sites' is one of the most obvious examples of how unhappy customers can find a voice online along with a worldwide audience willing to listen. The emergence of so called 'dot. complaint' talk-back sites such as eComplaints, Payusback and PlanetFeedback, is also symptomatic of the Net's two-way nature.

BE PREPARED

Ever since the chief financial officer of CNN confessed in 1999 that the company did not have an e-strategy, and subsequently caused CNN's share value to nosedive, businesses of all sizes and on both sides of the Atlantic have felt the need to formulate an e-strategy. However, many of these strategies have, to say the least, been misguided.

Although it has been disproven time and time again, the misguided mantra of 'If you build it, they will come,' has been the apparent logic behind many unvisited Web sites. The fact is, however, if you build it without a carefully thought out e-strategy, your site will be left stranded in the lay-by of the medium once referred to as the information super-highway.

Furthermore, there are a number of steps to take even before you start to formulate you e-strategy.

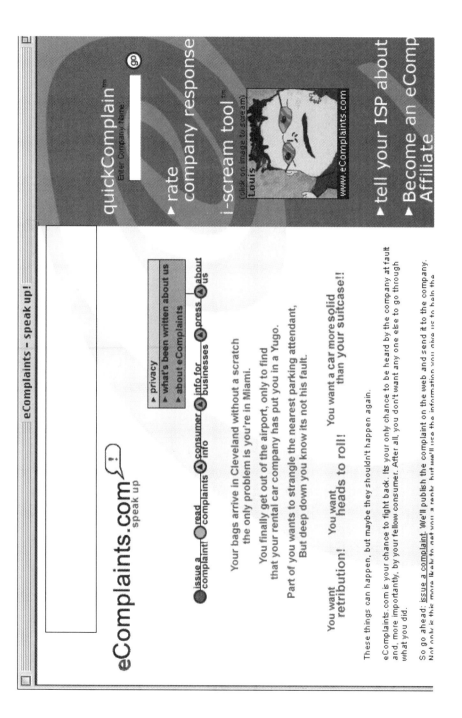

Figure 1.1 Ecomplaints.com: a complaint registry and resource site

Most important of all, you need to ensure that your business is, to use the appropriate jargon, e-ready.

To do this, you should undertake the following steps:

- **Establish where your business is today**. Before embarking online, revisit or write your business plan. While doing so, assess whether your unique selling points really are as unique as they once seemed. As will be discussed later on in this book, differentiation is the key to online success.

- **Do an 'e-audit'**. Look at every part of your business process from the viewpoint of reporting or displaying process information. It is important to take a close look at where the business goals can be delivered by (or interacted with) the Web.

Fulfilment is the key to online success

- **Review existing systems**. Before putting together an e-strategy it is advisable to look over your existing legacy systems and information (accounting, marketing databases etc). Examine and list all those parts of your business process where the customer comes into contact with your organization such as ordering, delivery, invoicing, customer support. It is important to think of how each of these areas can be integrated within your e-strategy.

- **Look at your supply chain**. Time and time again, in survey after survey, the one concern which is always voiced by potential online customers is that of fulfilment. Without having the assurance provided by going into a physical store and seeing the goods they are buying, they are always concerned about whether or not the product they order is going to be available, arrive on time, and in the right condition. If you use suppliers be sure that they will be able to alleviate these concerns. If they can't, you may have to look elsewhere.

ABOUT THIS BOOK

The purpose of this book is not simply to highlight the fundamental importance of having an e-strategy, but also to help you understand some of the factors which will determine the success of such a strategy. Given the fast-moving nature of this book's topic, it is important to realize that none of the advice or comment provided here is set in stone. The rules of business evolve and develop, and nowhere do these rules change faster than on the Internet.

That said, in its emphasis on broad principles rather than technical detail, it is hoped that many of the points made will hold true over time.

Specifically, the rest of the book will focus on the following areas:

- **Technology**. A brief assessment of the technological requirements for any e-business will be covered.

- **Design**. The principles of successful e-commerce design will be explored, with emphasis on a user-friendly approach.

- **Branding**. Although smaller companies believe brand strategies are best left to the big multinationals, on the Internet a strong, unique brand identity is essential if you are to differentiate your business from its competition.

- **Market identification**. E-business success depends on knowing exactly where, what and who your market is. Market knowledge is, if anything, more important online than it is in the real world.

- **Pricing**. If you intend to sell your products via the Web, there will be a number of pricing issues to consider, such as different currencies, comparison shopping and the danger of hiding costs.

- **Customer management**. On the Internet your customers are, to a greater or lesser extent, invisible. Chapter 7 looks at how to connect with these customers and meet their needs in Internet time. The emphasis will be on overcoming a major barrier to successful e-commerce – lack of trust. Related to this is the issue of fulfilment, both to domestic and international markets.

Connecting with the invisible customer

- **Promotion**. Search engine positioning, online PR and viral marketing will be all looked at as cost-effective alternatives to banner advertising.

- **Security**. This is a major issue for any business with an e-presence. Chapter 9 looks at the various ways businesses can protect their oper-ation from viruses, worms and hackers. Advice on how to alleviate the security concerns of online customers will also be included, as security fears act as one of the main factors preventing Web browsers from becoming Web shoppers.

- **Future trends**. The book will conclude with a look at developments taking place now which look set to impact on the future shape of e-business.

2

Starting out

A survey of small and medium-sized enterprises (SMEs), commissioned by Internet connectivity product provider 3Com, revealed that while many SMEs have a Web site, over three-quarters of them have no IT plan to further develop their Internet strategy, leaving them in danger of falling behind bigger businesses that are exploiting technology. Adrian Hurrel, UK managing director of 3Com concluded that, 'Our research clearly highlights that SMEs often feel very isolated because of a lack of knowledge about where to turn for advice and are wary that technology is too complex for their business to install and maintain.' As this chapter will show, the technology and knowledge required is accessible to businesses of every size.

ISPs

To conduct any form of business via the Internet, you will need an Internet service provider (ISP). An ISP acts as a 'middleman' providing you with the software needed for your modem to dial and connect to the Internet. Most also offer e-mail and Web hosting services (providing you with Web space required to set up your site). Choosing an ISP can prove to be a nightmare because there are thousands on the market. You must consider your ISP carefully because if you make the wrong decision it could damage your business. When considering an ISP you need to think about the following points very carefully:

Navigating the ISP nightmare

- **Reliability**. If a site is not accessible you need to know how long the repairs and maintenance will take.
- **Access**. If an ISP has slow download time (the time it takes for the Web site to appear on your customer's browser), customers will become frustrated with your company not the ISP.
- **Help**. Check the ISP has a reliable helpline before you sign up.
- **ISDN**. If you use an ISDN line make sure the ISP has the right access.

You will also need to decide whether you want your company to have broadband access, providing more powerful Internet connections. Despite the fact that broadband has not been snapped up by SMEs (around 80 per cent of UK businesses don't see the importance of it, according to Mori, 2001) the faster and more consistent your connection is, the more likely it is that it will save you money in the long term.

Business Internet magazines such as Internet Works (www.iwks.com) provide updated research on the top ISPs. Some reputable UK service providers include U-Net Limited (www.u-net.net), UUNET (www.uk.uu.net), CIX (www.cix.co.uk), Orbitalnet (www.orbitalnet.co.uk) and AAP InterNet (www.aapi.co.uk).

DOMAIN NAMES

If you want to be taken seriously on the Internet then you must purchase your own domain name rather than simply opting for a free online service such as those available at AOL or Compuserve. Your domain name should either be the name of your company such as Simons Bikes (www.simonsbikes.co.uk) or something relevant to your market such as The Bike Shop (www.thebikeshop.co.uk).

A Web site by any other name

When you are deciding what your domain name should be, also think of the suffix (the part that follows your company name). A suffix denotes what type of Web site you are or where you are from. For example, .fr is used for sites that are based in France. For further information on suffixes check the ICANN Web site (www.icann.org).

When you have decided on your Web site name register it at one of the following sites:

- Network Solutions (www.networksolutions.com). This site can help you find out who owns a domain name or change the registration details for your own domain name.

- Net Names (www.netnames.co.uk). You can search for .com, .co.uk or .net domains and have Net Names alert you when someone buys a similar address.

- Net Benefit (www.netbenefit.com). Net Benefit provides domain name registration, hosting and e-commerce services. Its I-Watch service informs you if someone registers a similar name.

- Nicnames (www.nicnames.co.uk). This is a UK and worldwide domain name registry. It is cheap and easy to use and you can search and buy domain names.

SELLING ONLINE

You don't need an especially powerful computer to run e-commerce software. In fact any mid-range business computer capable of running Windows and Internet Explorer will suffice. But it will need a large hard disk and lots of RAM (128 MB). Hosting services can be provided by your ISP, and for a domain name registration and 10 MB worth of space you will probably be looking at around £100 per year.

There are dozens of low-cost e-commerce solutions on the market, including:

- *Actinic Catalog* (www.actinic.co.uk). Actinic Catalog costs £349 and has an immense range of features and functions. It is specifically designed to enable SMEs to set up Internet sales channels and it is widely considered one of the simplest packages to use.

- *Actinic Business.* Actinic Business gives SMEs the means to extend their B2C (business-to-consumer) and B2B (business-to-business) operations to the Web quickly, easily and affordably. It is a complete tool-set for designing, building and managing online stores. It is also considered very good value for money.

- *Dragnet* (www.dragnet.co.uk). Dragnet E-Business Ltd. and Intelligent Network Technology (INT) can help you set up an e-commerce site for under £1,000. The package includes everything from hosting to online trading.

- Shop Creator (www.shopcreator.co.uk). Products range from around £200 and the site also offers a free software trial.

- Secure Trading (www.securetrading.com). Secure Trading offers real-time trading, high level security and fraud control.

- Worldpay (www.worldpay/com). Worldpay has a service called Click and Build which enables you to set up a merchant account with them in hours.

- Datacash (www.datacash.com). Datacash can quickly set up a merchant account for you enabling you to take transactions from most major credit cards.

- Netbanx (www.netbanx.com). Netbanx has several services and products that enable you to make transactions online.

London Symphony Orchestra and Royal Opera House

www.lso.co.uk   www.roh.org.uk

The London Symphony Orchestra (LSO) Web site went live in 1996 and began to offer ticket sales a couple of years later, thereby becoming the first UK orchestra to do so.

Selling tickets of orchestra performances via the Web involves a rather complex form of e-commerce. There may be only a small amount of individual events but there are many different dates, prices, discounts, seats and times of performance. The LSO used an off-the-shelf e-commerce solution and 10 per cent of total ticket sales now come from the Web. The Web site has proved especially helpful for overseas visitors and people from outside London.

As Tim Oldershaw, Web site coordinator of the LSO, says, 'we aim to give people as much information as possible and we recently added audio extracts and programme notes on performances. It's also very easy to include HTML directly within the item descriptions or in other places in the templates. This is a really good feature which means that I can easily achieve special effects, perhaps to draw attention to a particular concert or range of tickets without having any unexpected impact on other pages or on the rest of the site.' As all the work was done in-house it's not easy to calculate a complete return on investment but, as Tim remarks, 'it paid for itself almost immediately and has certainly been very well worth the modest purchase price.'

Another British institution with a worldwide cultural reputation is the Royal Opera House which used off the shelf e-commerce software to build their pilot site. Chris Bunce, the IT manager, said 'it was very easy and very quick and the total cost was less than £2,500.' This was considerably less than the estimated £25,000 and daily ticket requests are fairly steady at around 50 (which equates to approximately 2,000 tickets per month).

Both sites at first implemented a Web-based ticket request system, similar to existing fax and mail ordering, rather than real-time ticketing which would have been expensive to implement. Orders placed on the site are processed in a securely encrypted form.

Furthermore, the Royal Opera House has now moved to real-time ticketing. After extensive market research the organization have learnt that people prefer to know immediately whether their seats are available or not. As Bunce claims, 'this is particularly true of overseas visitors who are often putting together multiple engagements in a limited time frame.

Elizabeth Botham & Sons

www.botham.co.uk

Based in Whitby, Yorkshire, Elizabeth Botham & Sons is a traditional craft bakery that has been trading since 1865. The company was an early adopter of the Internet and it set up an e-commerce site in 1995, but only offers a fraction of the 400–500 sweet and savoury lines that are supplied each day for local outlets and wholesalers. Instead, the focus is on celebration cakes, biscuits, preserves, teas and coffees as well as hampers.

Recipes for e-commerce success

Botham is a classic example of a small business that has been able to widen its market and successfully harness the Internet as an additional sales channel. One factor that made the move to the Web easier was that the company was already using mail order.

In its lifespan the Botham Web site has already undergone several changes. At first it made no provision for secure ordering. Instead customers simply ordered goods by printing out a form that they faxed with their credit card details.

However, this was replaced by a SSL (Secure Socket Layer) system which encrypted orders complete with credit card and address details. But as the managing director, Michael Jarman explains: 'the SSL system was relatively inflexible for editing products or updating prices.'

The company then chose to buy an off-the-shelf e-commerce package which could handle the whole process of catalogue management, order processing and stock monitoring. This also provides secure encryption of card details and allows the company to process orders in-house.

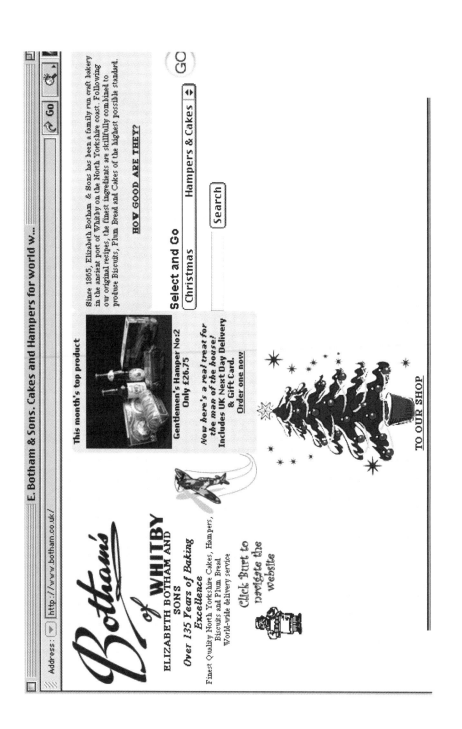

Figure 2.1 Botham's used the Internet to widen their market

PRINCIPLES OF GOOD WEB DESIGN

There is no one answer to the question 'What makes a good Web site?' It simply depends on what you want a Web site to achieve. However, having said that, there are some universal design principles for e-business sites which most Web designers and developers would find hard to disagree with. Whether you are outsourcing your Web design activity, using an in-house team or a DIY Web building tool it will prove helpful to understand these principles.

First and foremost among these is straightforward navigation. As Jakob Nielsen, arguably the most well-known and respected Web design expert, has reiterated on numerous occasions, efficient navigation and usability is equally important to every Internet user.

To understand what makes a good site, it is important to look at the very human way the Web is put together. The Internet works as a form of *bricolage*: Web designers often create things out of whatever is lying about. This opportunism, according to *The New York Times'* David Weinberger, 'makes the Web unpredictable, creative and always the result of human hands.' The problem with a lot of sites, therefore, is that they fail to take the fundamental nature of the Internet into consideration. They are all too often very predictable, uncreative and inhuman. There is, after all, nothing very human about the average company brochure.

Replicating the Internet within your site

Considering content

As most people access a Web site to find information, not to be bowled over by flashy graphics, the way content is put together and presented should be carefully considered.

After all, site visitors do not want to be burdened with screen after screen of unbroken text. Information therefore needs to be presented in an accessible and user-friendly way, which doesn't require too much effort on the part of the user. There are a number of ways to make your content digestible. Firstly, you can break text up into short bite-sized chunks, divided by frequent sub-headings. Visitors will then be able to scan the screen for information of use to them. You can also link to more in-depth material, making sure that users can decide what they want to know more about by providing links at the foot of text-bites (think of how information-packed portal sites present their information). Also, for a Web site to present information in a user-friendly format no one page of your site should ever be more than three clicks away from any other page. Straightforward links are another help. Many otherwise successful sites are burdened with confusing and obscure links. Although clever icons and imaginative wording may seem like a good idea, when it comes to links it's always better to call a spade a spade. Stick to easily identifiable links such as 'Home', 'New', 'Contact', 'Product Information' and 'About this site'.

Then there is the question of where your content should come from. If you plan to update your site's information on a regular basis – and ideally you should – the task of creating content can become increasingly hard work.

One way to get around this is to ask visitors to contribute content to your site. In doing this you will also be able to engage them at a deeper level and

I link, therefore I am

make your site more objective. Amazon makes good use of this approach by asking visitors to submit book reviews.

Another option is to hire a company to supply you with suitable content. Syndicated content is becoming increasingly popular with e-commerce sites wanting to provide their visitors with a one-stop information shop. The way it works is simple: you pay a company (such as the US-based Screaming Media) for a news feed and it provides you with up-to-date stories relevant to your site. No matter how 'niche' your online audience is, content providers will be able to supply the relevant information.

If you want to update your site's content yourself, there are a number of content management systems which make the task as simple as possible. Tools such as Active Server Pages or Cold Fusion are often used to develop highly functional sites that can be easily maintained. These content management systems give you access to site maintenance through a browser window and don't require installation of any new software.

Harness your pulling power

Finally, it is important to realize that unless a Web site is offering something of real value to potential clients or customers, it is unlikely to generate repeat visits. The Internet is, according to marketing jargon, a 'pull' as opposed to a 'push' medium. This means that Internet users have to seek out information and pull it towards them. To do this they need to have a strong enough reason. Exclusive information and advice is one way to draw people to your site, especially if this information can be tailored to an individual user's specific needs.

WEB DESIGN OUTSOURCING

If you decide to outsource your Web design here are some questions you should ask the designers before taking the plunge:

Interrogating your designer

- Can I see your other work? Take a look at their work and make sure that all their sites have clear navigation and are not graphic intensive – an easy way to spot a beginner.

- What will you expect me to do? Planning is very time consuming and some agencies will only build what you've specified whereas others provide considerable assistance in developing an Internet strategy with you.

- Will you advise me on an e-commerce system? Make sure they offer you the right e-commerce system and not just their standard solution.

- Who owns the completed sites? If you can believe it, some Web sites don't belong to the companies who have paid for them.

- Are there ongoing costs? There may be hidden annual charges and undisclosed additional costs.

- What are the payment terms? Make sure you know how they will charge and when you will be required to pay.

- How long will it take? Agree a timetable to work to and make sure the design agency sticks to it.

- How will I maintain my site? Find out how much it will cost or whether you can do it yourself.

A list of Web designers can be found at the UK Web designers site (www.ukwebdesigners.net).

TECHNOLOGICAL INTEGRATION

It is best to follow the old KISS (keep it simple, stupid) principle when deciding on all your technical requirements. Look at the way work flows into and through the company from the initial enquiry through to delivery and invoicing. Elaborate technical solutions are not always required to deliver what appear to be complex Web services. The main area of frustration is real-time integration and there are a number of applications on the market that can help in this area.

You may also consider using an applications service provider (ASP) which enable companies to avoid having to pay large sums of money on technology and IT staff in order to set up or expand an e-business. E-business service providers (ESPs) are advancements on the ASP model and concentrate on the infrastructure that applications need to run reliably and securely.

ESPs provide software, hardware and technical support that e-businesses require to start or improve their trading on the Internet, including Internet connection from multiple ISPs, Web site and e-commerce engines and CRM (customer relationship management) systems. One such ESP is AppTapp (www.apptapp.com).

Back-end integration – another way

www.laterooms.com

Late Rooms was launched in November 1999 and cost about £70,000. The site helps hotels from around the world sell their late availability bedrooms, and customers take advantage of those savings. Instead of opting for real-time integration of hotel systems into the site's back-end, an administration area was built which allows hotel owners to register and maintain their details online via a standard Web interface. In November 1999, 250 hotels were listed and now that number stands at an impressive 6,000.

GETTING ADVICE

As 40 per cent of companies are currently unsure of where to find expert or impartial advice to guide them in developing an e-business strategy (according to a 2001 Institute of Management report), the Technology Means Business (TMB) scheme from the Department of Trade and Industry (DTI) may be of interest. The scheme aims to provide an industry standard for the accreditation of business information and information technology advice to small businesses. The TMB site (www.technologymeansbusiness.org.uk) has a list of accredited advisers and 14 accreditation centres throughout the UK. As Patricia Hewitt, the Minister for Small Business and E-commerce said, 'Technology Means Business enables companies to identify accredited business advisers and be confident they are getting the best advice on how the latest information and communication technologies can benefit their business.'

3

Your e-brand

For many people branding is associated with huge global companies and their world dominating signi-fiers – the Nike swoosh, the golden arches of McDonalds, the musical-inspired Gap ads. When they place themselves up against consumer giants such as these, many businesses may be tempted to believe that a successful brand strategy, however attractive the idea may be, is simply beyond their resources. This opinion is certainly held by Daniel Squirrel, CEO of eMagazineshop.com, who believes that 'branding is more significant for multinational companies who can allocate huge budgets to build a brand.'

Branding is essential to every e-business

Indeed, if branding is all about multimillion dollar advertising campaigns and worldwide recognition, then most businesses would be quite right to focus on other areas. The fact is, however, that there is more to branding than big dollar advertising and promotional drives. At its most basic level, branding is about one thing and one thing alone – *differentiation*. It is the way in which a business presents its difference to its potential customers, a way of telling the market 'this is what we stand for.' Think of Volvo and the brand value that comes to mind is 'safety', think of Marks and Spencer and the triumvirate of 'quality, value and service' will probably be the most obvious brand association.

On the Internet, branding becomes even more important. This is because once you are situated within a medium often characterized by 'information overload', differentiation is everything. Furthermore, while in the real world your market may be defined in terms of geography, on the Internet *all* your competitors – even those with real world bases thousands of miles away – are now only a few clicks away from your site.

If you are transferring your business online you therefore need to look at those qualities which make you a success offline, and accentuate and emphasize them on your Web site. However, as the Internet is an interactive medium, the development of your brand should not be decided by your company alone, but by interactivity or (to use the e-marketeer's favourite buzz word) *dialogue* between the company and its target audience.

COMMUNITY BUILDING

While e-branding is about differentiation, its main aim must be customer loyalty. After all, without feeling any sense of loyalty to your site your customers will be unlikely to make that all important second visit.

Whereas in the early days of e-commerce the emphasis was on increasing the number of 'eyeballs' (unique site visits), it soon became clear that the constant pursuit of new custom was more expensive that generating repeat visits. Indeed, many of the highest profile dot.com casualties (mentioning no names, of course), were doomed because of their obsession with brand awareness over brand loyalty.

One of the most effective ways in which the Internet can be used to generate this loyalty is via online communities. 'The Internet is about brand depth, not breadth,' says Rory Sutherland, executive creative director of marketing company Ogilvy One. 'Once you have your loyal community, there are fabulous opportunities for cross selling, personalized services and meeting the multiple needs of the same group.' Listening to customers and letting customers listen to each other means that goals can be achieved sooner rather than later.

E-mail, chat rooms, discussion boards, guest books and electronic newsletters have all been used by companies wanting to transform their e-business into a profitable e-community.

Indeed, the successful online brands such as Amazon, Ebay, Yahoo! and MSN have always realized that if visitors can interact with each other, it not only increases their loyalty to a site but it also enables the brand to develop in line with the consumer. Indeed, customer opinions voiced in online forums have often led to a complete rethinking of a company's marketing strategy.

For instance, when Amazon was recently toying with the idea of variable pricing, it decided to trial run the policy on its DVD products. Within a week Amazon had reversed this strategy, as it had received a negative response within its DVD Talk chat forum.

Of course, chat rooms don't make sense for every business, as not every site can guarantee that there will be always enough visitors in conversation-mood. However, by using free bulletin-board software (see Webboard.oreilly.com) or even an e-mailing list, companies can engage in conversation with their customers and listen to their suggestions.

SITES FOR SORE EYES

Although your Internet activity is unlikely to be limited to your Web site alone, there can be little doubt that it will be the focus point of your online activity.

If your customers are left confused after a click around your site, then there is little hope for your brand. In a sea of information, sites which are simple and user-friendly are invariably the ones Internet users welcome on their Web browsers.

As a general rule, the more 'stripped down' a Web site's design is, the better. It is generally agreed that two or three dominant colours are all that is needed to create a consistent brand identity – the 'rainbow effect' caused by an over-abundance of colours should be avoided at all costs. As Web users want to absorb information on a Web page in as short a time as possible, text and images should be used with strict restraint throughout a Web site.

Likewise, simple, straightforward navigation is one of the most essential aspects in determining the success of an e-brand. After all, if a trip to a site leaves people dazed and confused they are unlikely to come back.

Generally speaking, net users like familiarity. They like to be able to recognize links in an instant, and become frustrated when presented with obscure icons and cryptic commands. Links with self-explanatory titles such as 'Home', 'Contact', and 'News' may seem boring, but they avoid confusion. If you want to exercise your linguistic ingenuity, link commands are not the place to do it. Another way to make navigation straightforward is to follow the 'three-click' rule. This states that no single Web page should be more than three clicks, or links, away from any other within the same site.

However, while familiarity is important in terms of navigation, for your brand to stand out the other elements of your site must be unique. The most obvious way to express your company's unique brand values is in the text of your site.

The problem here is that Internet users do not 'read' text on the Web – at least not in the traditional left-to-right sense – they scan it. This fact emerged in the late-1990s when Sun Microsystems (the US company that promoted the Internet hardest in the mid-1990s) conducted extensive research into how people absorb information on the Internet. They discovered that in most cases people scan the screen, searching at speed for relevant text or images. People therefore do not want to be bombarded with screen after screen of unbroken text.

Adopting usability guidelines

Jakob Nielsen, the man behind the Sun research and author of the best-selling *Designing and Usability*, proposed a series of guidelines for making text more in tune with the way people actually use the Internet and thereby avoiding information overload. This included: breaking text into bite-sized chunks (containing only one single idea), using frequent sub-headings, highlighting keywords and using bullet points. Where a lot of information needs to be conveyed he maintains that it is always best to spread it over a few pages than to put a lot of text on a single page.

Simplicity of design is particularly important when it comes to e-commerce sites. Research shows that most online 'shopping carts' are ditched before reaching the checkout. One of the main reasons for this is the amount of effort required by the potential customer. Extensive form-filling can certainly complicate and lengthen the e-shopping experience. One solution is to store information so that visitors only have to fill in forms on their first visit. Other ways the e-commerce process can be simplified include isolating order buttons and enabling users to view their shopping cart contents.

By keeping the site design as simple as possible, you will enable your customers to concentrate on your brand message itself.

BEYOND LOGOS

While your Web site must be the main focus of your e-branding efforts it is important to realize that branding does not just relate to the visual appearance of the site, but involves every aspect of your Web presence. 'Branding goes further than logo,' says Graham Wright, co-founder of health product site Medicare. User-friendly navigation, he claims, has been the most important factor in the success of Medicare's e-branding (initially set up for a modest £700 but at the time of writing anticipating an annual turnover of £250,000).

This is affirmed by Dave Holden, Creative Director of WebShed who remarks that 'usability and usefulness are the key points.' Although Web designers (whether in-house or out-house) are rarely responsible for the whole reputation of a company, they do have a significant role to play. For instance, in the notorious case of Boo.com it was the site's fundamental design problems – its very lack of usefulness – which undermined the multi-million dollar marketing campaign and caused the most damage to the brand identity that the campaign had sought to build.

The other design issue to take on board is that it must not create a false impression of your company. Owing to the feedback culture of the Internet, it is important to realize that branding cannot mislead. As Jeremy Hamilton from M-Corp, puts it, 'branding is very significant but you can't buy it, you have to live it.'

Branding, he claims, is about an attitude of mind based on 'trust, respect and an intuitive grasp of what a company stands for.' In other words, the Web site design itself must reflect the reality of the customer's experience.

BRAND PROTECTION

Not only can the Internet help build brands, it can also play a part in their destruction.

It is a fact that the Internet enables customers to get their point across. The question is whether or not they will do it via a company's own Web site or through an online forum such as Ciao.com or Epinions.com. When customers really feel neglected they sometimes even set up 'suck' sites dedicated to attacking the brand or company in question.

Microsoft and McDonalds may be the most obvious victims of hostile consumer activism online but even smaller companies can easily become targets. The fact that people can disguise their identity online means that competitors and aggrieved customers can spread misinformation about your company in chat rooms and discussion boards.

Going back to Internet guru Esther Dyson's comment at a London Business School seminar (quoted in Chapter 2): 'Things are two-way now. Readers are talking back to newspapers, vendors to buyers and citizens to governments'. As a result of this feedback potential, some analysts have declared that the Internet poses a threat to the sanctity of the brand. After all, customers are no longer simply consumers but brand flag-wavers – and as they are not on the pay-roll they are under no obligation to toe the company's line.

The only way to protect your online brand is to accept this state of affairs and deal with it. This means rather than ignore the fact that people are able to speak their mind on the Internet, embrace it. Incorporate customer opinion on your site, provide easy online contacts (eg links to relevant e-mail addresses), respond to criticism. Most important of all, Web sites must deliver on their promises. If a company promises to get products to their customers' doorsteps within 24 hours, word will get around if it takes twice as long.

Indeed, some online consumers could be forgiven for thinking that some e-commerce sites seem to operate in dog years, such is the discrepancy between the delivery time stated and the delivery time actually achieved. Also, if there is a problem, don't try and ostrich out of the situation. If you don't tell customers about any mishaps, you can rest assured other customers will do it for you.

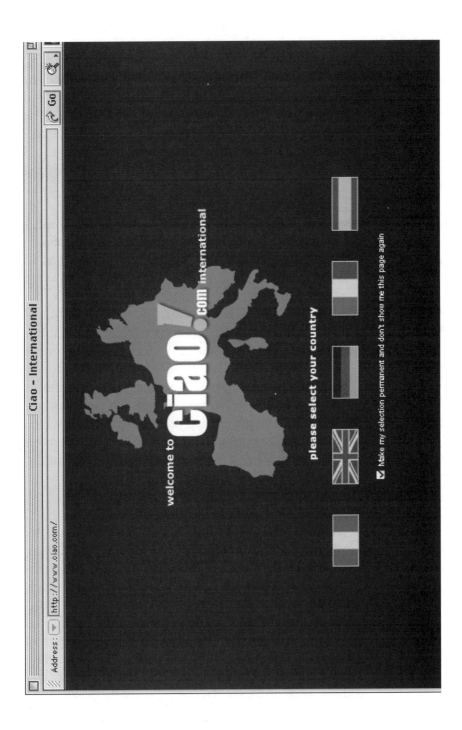

Figure 3.1 Customers are able to voice their opinions at Ciao.com

THE NEW BRAND POWER

The Internet offers a substantial medium for branding, but to compare the branding power of the Internet to that of television is inaccurate. The Internet offers a new kind of branding based on interactivity. This is truly something that traditional broadcast media does not offer. In addition, the Internet allows for awareness studies that can be completed faster than ever before.

As the Internet is an interactive, user-initiated medium, Internet brand builders must also be exceptional listeners, especially since digital consumers are no longer passive recipients of marketing messages.

Understand the power of connected markets

'On the Internet, markets are getting more connected and more powerfully vocal every day,' says David Weinberger, co-author of the highly influential *The Cluetrain Manifesto*, 'every product you can name, from fashion to office supplies, can be discussed, argued over, researched and brought as part of a vast conversation among the people interested in it.' The powerful e-brands are the ones which are willing to engage and move with this conversation, encouraging feedback to help direct the brand forward. Therefore, rather than making the fate of a brand unpredictable, the Internet can be (and indeed, is being) used to eliminate the guesswork.

Ultimately, the brand is the perception of the company, and this is formed not only by 'usefulness' but also by the values of that company. It is important then for you to get a handle on what your company and its brand signifies to customers. This means identifying the core audience at the very beginning. As M-Corp's Jeremy Hamilton puts it, 'perception of brands is different to different people, so the starting point is to focus on the target customers, particularly their needs and expectations.'

4

The market

At the risk of stating the obvious, it should be pointed out that for a business to succeed online it needs an online market. For businesses successfully ticking over in the real world, the online market for their products or services may seem obvious. In many cases, the offline and online markets may even seem to be one and the same.

This assumption should be avoided. Although there is normally an overlap between the type of customers a business attracts offline and those it secures via the Web, often there are considerable differences. Most obviously, these differences are geographic. For instance, a UK specialist record store in Cambridge may be limited by its real world location, but on the Web it can attract music lovers from Los Angeles to Tokyo.

There may be other differences too. For instance, in the real world your business may attract a cross-section of the general public. On the Internet it is often better for businesses, especially smaller businesses, to narrow down and focus on one niche market. This way they can build a strong reputation among a key fraction of the Internet population. Indeed, many of the e-commerce pioneers who managed to get rich early on in the dot.com gold rush were niche market-eers. Model railways, Scotch whisky, Cuban cigars, spicy chilli sauce, dolls' houses – all were used as the basis for highly successful niche Web sites. In fact, it's hard to imagine any site failing because it's too *niche*, unless you are planning to set up a site aimed solely at left-handed yak farmers. Even then, you shouldn't rule it out.

Left-handed yak farmers may be out of luck

DEFINE YOUR MARKET

Although it may seem the most obvious principle of any e-strategy, many companies have failed to identify the specific requirements of the online market they target. Indeed, many of the high profile online failures were targeting markets that didn't yet and (in some cases, at least) may never exist. For instance, many of the B2B exchanges have failed to generate trade owing to the fact that certain industries (eg agriculture) are not ready for online business transactions.

Similarly, bricks-and-mortar companies feeling the need to establish a Web presence have often rushed into the 'whole hog' option without considering whether that is right for their established market. As Jeremy Hamilton, an e-business strategist at M-Corp observes, 'the past few years have seen many corporates rush to have an online presence, developing into the e-commerce side of things. However, many smaller organizations have now recognized that it is more appropriate to offer a suite of online pre- and post-sales service and support tools, prior to implementing an online sales facility.'

That said, there are an equal number of companies with Web sites still consisting of nothing more than 'brochureware', who are missing out on a clear e-commerce opportunity. So the first task is to work out whether or not there is a market, secondly to decipher who exactly that market is and then to decide whether or not that market will expect to complete transactions via the Web site. Once these decisions have been made, you face the more specific task of presenting your site to the target market in a way which appeals to them.

Of course, there are some universal principles. As usability guru Jakob Nielsen has reiterated many times, efficient navigation is important to practically every Internet user. Security, fulfilment and privacy issues also need to be tackled regardless of the target market.

But after that, it really does depend on the target audience. A site targeting over-50s (the so-called silver surfers) based in the UK Home Counties is clearly going to have different design objectives to a site aimed at click-happy, MP3-trading Limp Bizkit fans in Louisiana. These differences are, most obviously, going to impact on areas such as the visual layout of the site as each different audience is likely to have different aesthetic values. By looking at the type of online and offline media that relevant

Internet users are currently surrounding themselves with, companies can get a good idea of the right visual 'language' to apply.

But as Dave Holden, Creative Director at WebShed acknowledges, 'when it comes to targeting audiences the visual appearance of the Web site is not the most important thing.' As many sexy looking dot.com failures have shown, beauty is only screen-deep and not necessarily the best basis for a long-term relationship with a target market.

More important is the real value and relevance that the site offers its market. And, of course, this relevance can only be determined once you have decided not only who your target customer is (in terms of gender, age, lifestyle etc.) but *where* he or she is based.

INTERNATIONAL MARKETS

Although your offline business may only cater for a domestic market, the Web offers you the potential to cast a wider net.

By setting up shop on the Web, a company is immediately accessible by people from across the globe. As Phil Scanlan, CEO of translation services provider WorldLingo (www.worldlingo.com) observes, the Internet offers various basic advantages for companies seeking a global presence. Scanlan explains: 'A Web site is a window to the world, where people can see what products and services you offer wherever and whenever they want to.'

Moreover, the Internet has greatly increased the rate of cross-border shopping. IDC's Project Atlas Survey of 25,000 Web users worldwide has shown that those who shop on the Web from home do 4.5 per cent of their shopping outside their native country.

Therefore, Web sites that are able to attract multi-lingual, multicultural audiences are fast becoming must-have requirements, rather than luxurious options. However, the issues involved in attracting global audiences are complex and extend far beyond language options and currency converters.

The motto for international marketing always used to be 'think global, act local'. When the Internet was first adopted for commercial purposes in the mid-1990s many people believed this marketing mantra no longer applied.

Among them was Nigel Pleasants, marketing author and CEO of The Watershed Partners, a network of sales and marketing executives that facilitate the successful entry of European Web companies into American markets. 'When the Web offered us the opportunity to market globally from a single Web site, I thought the paradigm was finally broken' he admits. 'Now we could think *and* act globally from the comfort of our own domains.'

Of course, this perception ultimately led to the rise in the dot.com death toll as more and more companies realized they had cast their net too wide. As Shonna Keegan, director of corporate communications at Register.com has put it 'one size does not fit all, even in the same language group'.

Boo.com

One of the main factors which contributed to the speedy demise of the notorious online clothes store Boo.com was the decision to launch in 19 different countries simultaneously. A similar advertising campaign and identical Web site for each national market may have seemed like a good way to unify a global brand identity, but this costly and misguided strategy has subsequently become the archetypal 'how not to' example for businesses seeking to attract global audiences.

Thinking local, acting global

Boo.com may be the most obvious case, but there are numerous other examples of how a failure to acknowledge national, cultural and linguistic differences has resulted in serious problems for global companies. Often these examples offer valuable lessons regarding the pitfalls that can be encountered. For instance, when Yahoo!'s auction service was accused of violating French law (for allowing French Internet users access to pages offering Nazi memorabilia for auction) it highlighted the need to involve local individuals and organizations who understand the specific legal issues which may emerge.

Many sites have also discovered that domain names may not always translate well into other languages. The US gift company, GetGift.com has had difficulty in penetrating the Scandinavian market owing to the fact that Get Gift translates as 'Goat Poison' in Swedish and Norwegian. Likewise, the ill-fated online invitation service Evite.com found its globalization efforts were thwarted because 'evite' means 'avoid' in many of the Romance languages.

A LEVEL PLAYING FIELD

Another advantage of the Internet is that it levels the playing field and makes international business an option for almost any type of business. As Simon Usher, chief executive of Webdesign and marketing company Reading Room (www.readingroom.net) points out, 'the size of the company is not as important as the global possibilities of the product. For instance, a small English company selling Victoriana and Georgian memorabilia might find huge potential in Japan and the United States.'

This view is echoed by Oliver Davies, projects director at international Web design agency Hildebrand Interactive (www.hildebrandinteractive.com). He observes that, 'The Internet makes it possible for smaller operators with more flexible management structures to challenge larger players without incurring the costs normally associated with building a global business.'

INCREASED COMPETITION

The flipside of this argument is that domestic-based online companies of all sizes now face increased competition from overseas. Once you are on the Web, you are competing not only with a rival business across the street, but with competitors from all over the globe. In order to compete successfully businesses need to make sure that their online activity is relevant to every market they target.

Once a business decides to use the Internet to target foreign markets, it first needs to consider which ones to go after. It is important to concentrate only on one or two markets at a time, rather than spread resources too finely in the first instance, as many failed dot.coms can testify (see the Boo.com case study above).

'Businesses must ensure their products, platforms and operational models are suited to the new market,' according to Ije Nwokorie from Ion Global (www.ion-global.com), an international e-consultancy that creates multilingual Web sites. There are no markets which are more suited to UK companies than others, it simply depends on the type of products or services you have on offer.

PARLEZ-VOUS DOT.COM? – SPEAKING YOUR MARKET'S LANGUAGE

Although it may seem sensible to concentrate on English-speaking markets first, many UK Internet companies have found US markets difficult to crack owing to the amount of competition they face from domestic Web sites. Furthermore, most of the countries with the fastest growing numbers of online shoppers, such as those in South America, Asia and mainland Europe, do not have English as a first language. So, while English remains the most popular language for e-commerce sites to use, it is not sufficient for sites focusing on global markets.

According to research findings from Global Reach (www.globalreach.com), 52.5 per cent of the online population currently access the Internet in a language other than English, and this figure is set to increase to 75 per cent by 2005. These findings are even more significant when viewed in conjunction with research conducted by IDC, which found that customers are four times more likely to purchase on the Internet if a company pitches in their own language.

The conclusion to be drawn is simple: if an e-business only communicates in English on the Net, it is placing a language barrier between itself and more than 50 per cent of its potential market.

'One of the easiest ways to convert browsers into shoppers is to ensure that they can read the site in a language that they understand,' says Simon Brooks, global marketing director for WorldPay (www.worldpay.com), the e-commerce solutions company providing global payment processing systems. 'Without easy access to the right information in a language they understand, shoppers are more likely to go in search of an alternative supplier,' he adds.

Despite this fact, e-commerce businesses of all sizes have so far been slow to offer multilingual options. Merrill Lynch claims that only about 10 per cent of e-businesses that trade across borders have any serious plans for coordinating and maintaining their Web sites across multiple languages.

Even among those companies that do provide different language options on their Web site, most fail to respond to foreign language e-mail enquiries. Research from WorldLingo suggests that only one out of 250 companies respond to a foreign language e-mail within six hours and only 8 per cent respond at all.

In other words, companies are losing customers because they are not providing the level of communication and interaction required by foreign visitors in order for them to make a purchase. The apparent problem seems to be that companies either do not recognize the need or are unaware of the solutions available to them.

It's true that multilingual sites often increase the technological demands that e-commerce companies face. As WorldPay's Simon Brooks points out, 'Some languages, Japanese for example, require script to be unicoded in order to support a multilingual Web site.' With 2,200 world languages, the reluctance many companies have is perhaps understandable. However, it is worth noting that only 10 languages account for 90 per cent of the languages spoken on the Internet – English, French, Italian, German, Spanish, Portuguese, Russian, Chinese, Japanese and Korean.

Getting to grips with 2,200 world languages

A HELPING HAND

There are a number of companies which now provide specialized software and services to make it easy for e-business to communicate and do business internationally. For instance, UK-based WorldLingo offers a variety of machine and human translation services for a wide range of international companies.

These services include an instant Web site translator which enables users to view a Web site in 10 languages, a commercial e-mail translator, an international domain registry service and a resource of over 4,000 qualified bilingual native speakers who provide professional translations in over 40 languages.

The content management systems Vignette (www.vignette.com) and Red Snapper (www.red snapper.com) have both proved successful at managing multilingual content (they can handle double byte characters such as those used in Asian languages). There is also a 'Starter Package' service provided by Global Reach that's aimed at small companies. The package translates your home page into three languages and registers your site in the 20 top indexes for each language zone.

The Royal National Institute for Deaf People (RNID)

www.rnidshop.com

The Royal National Institute for Deaf People (RNID) set up its e-commerce store at the end of 2000. The Internet empowers people with hearing loss to buy products and services and find the information they need. Gone are the difficulties of telephone conversations or face-to-face contact.

The Web site has attracted a number of orders from countries in the EU including France, Germany and Greece. At present people from outside the EU cannot buy from the site. 'Selling outside the EU complicates matters,' says Martin Bottomley, the RNID Web manager. 'For example, no VAT is due and there are issues with fraud from certain areas of the world. This is a problem for small Internet merchants like us as we are liable for fraudulent credit card use. I believe it is a huge issue that the European Commission should be dealing with.'

However, you can argue that the risks are no worse than with mail order or any other transaction where the cardholder isn't present.

Another reason to limit sales geographically in the short term is potential problems with selling electrical goods – only some can be sold abroad. 'Of course we can resolve many of these issues, but we thought first of all it would be sensible to limit ourselves to the EU, with plans to offer worldwide sales in the next six months or so,' explains Martin. 'Also we had no idea what level of orders we would get and wanted to avoid difficulties in fulfilment if we were flooded with sales.'

Martin Bottomley is planning to work on getting a more precise profile of the customers buying from the Web in future. 'That is our next step but we didn't want to put people off the purchasing process by asking them lots of questions while they were online, so we are planning to e-mail questionnaires instead. We will also collate more detailed traffic analysis. Then we can focus the site and our marketing more precisely'.

The consensus of opinion among e-business experts is that, if budgets permit, a site for each market is best. Sites such as Amazon and Yahoo! have all shown how companies can maintain a coherent identity while keeping content relevant to each market they target. Other companies, such as Ciao.com, Durex and fashion retailer Haburi, have separate sites linked to one home page (usually with a .com suffix).

Although cultural differences need to be acknowledged, it is inadvisable to pass off a Web site as American or French if the content is produced in London. Indeed, there are many instances when accentuating the country of origin may actually be a bonus. For instance, Inverness-based manufacturer of Scotch whisky, The Whisky Shop, acknowledges that Scottishness helps sell its products abroad. While its UK site (www.whiskyshop.com) concentrates solely on the quality of the product, its US site (www.whiskyshopusa.com) incorporates evocative Highland imagery.

However, the secret to targeting markets successfully is to target one market at at time. So although, the Web does enable you to reach a global audience, it can benefit you to establish yourself in your local market before looking further afield. Not only does this help you establish your e-business, a local approach can also verify that there is a market for your idea.

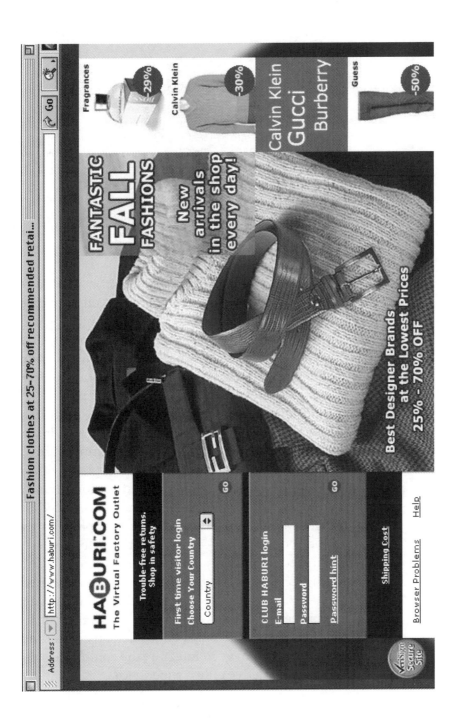

Figure 4.1 The online discount fashion retailer Haburi provides different language options for its international audience

Justabeep

www.justabeep.com

Justabeep.com, a provider of SMS marketing services to bars and nightclubs, ran a three-month trial in Glasgow which has resulted in a very strong local brand presence. The company proved its concept worked in Glasgow and is now planning to launch into the rest of the UK.

ADDING VALUE

When you are researching your market, you should realize that there is a difference between knowing who you are targeting and successfully doing so. The only way to ensure that your e-strategy is a successful one is by not only knowing who your products or services appeal to, but also how you are going to get these people to come to your site.

To succeed in the information age, businesses need to provide *information*

As Stuart Melhuish, CEO for Amaze Ltd, has pointed out, 'UK companies are coming to a more mature understanding of business transactions, instead of seeing them as solely taking place within the economic sphere.' It may sound obvious, but to succeed in the Information Age, businesses need to provide *information*. The majority of people who go online, both in the UK and worldwide, are not looking to shop. They are, in general, looking for solutions to problems and answers to questions. They certainly do not want to click through screen after screen of fatuous self-praise. If a Web site is to cast a wider net and reach out to as many people as possible, it will have to integrate the commerce side into an informative online experience.

The information your site provides needs to be appropriate to the products you sell. If you sell aromatherapy oils, for instance, you could provide an A–Z of health problems followed by a suitable remedy. This would be a great way of incorporating the aromatherapy products you sell into the information the site visitor requires. Tailored content is the secret to satisfying information hunger. The more interactive a site is, the more each site visit is a unique and personal experience. Equally, it follows that the more you know your online audience, the more relevant the material throughout the site will be.

RESEARCHING YOUR ONLINE MARKET

The best place to start researching your online market is, unsurprisingly, on the Internet. By looking at the Web sites of your competitors, you will be able to see what they are doing well and not so well, as well as work out the difference between what they are doing and your own online activity.

The Google search engine (www.google.com or .co.uk) is probably the most useful tool when conducting competitor research. By simply typing in the name of the competitor company into the search box, you will be able to find not only the company's Web site but also all the mentions of that company on other online sources. Among the other useful search engines are AltaVista (www.altavista.co.uk), Excite (www.excite.co.uk), Lycos (www.lycos.com) and NorthernLight (www.northernlight.com). There are also meta-search engines such as Mamma (www.mamma.com) and MetaCrawler (www.meta crawler.com) which search many of the most popular search engines simultaneously.

You can also conduct primary research by inter-acting with your customers online, whether via e-mail or your Web site. More information on online customer research can be found in Chapter 8.

5

Money matters

Although many businesses initially build a Web site
to promote their offline operation, after a while they
start to realize that they are missing out on a real
opportunity to generate extra revenues. By adding
an e-commerce element to your Internet strategy,
you may be able to reach out to a completely new
audience of customers. However, if you do decide to
sell your own products online, there are a number of
points to consider, particularly relating to pricing.

As this chapter will show, selling your own
products online is not the only way to generate Web
revenue. Banner advertising, sponsorships and
affiliate schemes all offer genuine money-making
possibilities for those businesses with a strong Web
presence.

SELLING PRODUCTS ONLINE

If you sell tangible goods offline, it is quite likely that you will also be able to sell them online. However, to do so you will not only need to invest in secure server technology, but also make sure that your merchant status covers you for online credit card transactions.

Establishing a transaction system

The easiest and most effective way to take orders is to establish a transaction system that sends customer details straight to the credit card issuer. This means the order can be verified straight away. To learn more about transaction systems visit Verifone (www.verifone.com) or WebSockets (www.websockets.com), both of which offer transaction related software products.

AFFILIATE SCHEMES

Although selling its products and services may be the most obvious way a business can bring in revenues via its Web site, it is not the only way. A growing number of Web sites opt in to affiliate schemes whereby they can help sell another companies' products and gain a percentage of any sales made.

The first affiliate scheme, and still the most popular, was set up by Amazon in July 1996. Amazon founder Jeff Bezos had the idea that instead of simply having a few sites link to his site's home page, it would make perfect sense for all parties involved if these sites helped promote and sell Amazon products, and gained a commission on every sale. Bezos was right, and now his company has half a million affiliates situated across the globe. In fact, affiliate marketing now accounts for 25 per cent of all transactions made on the Web.

However, if you are looking to incorporate affiliate marketing within your e-strategy it is important to be realistic. As you will be only making between 5 and 15 per cent on all product sold, it is unlikely that you will be able to depend on it as your main source of online income. But, as the process of becoming an affiliate is a relatively simple one (it often involves little more than cutting and pasting a chunk of HTML from the affiliate host), it can be a cost-effective way to boost revenue.

Cut and paste an affiliate solution

In order to make sure that you don't devalue your site, however, it is essential that you choose a relevant and trustworthy affiliate host. After all, the fact that you don't have to handle orders also means that you are putting the reputation of your business in another person's hands. It may even be worthwhile placing a sample order yourself before inviting your site users to do the same. Trust takes time to build online and, when lost, can often be impossible to restore.

If you want to see the types of companies offering affiliate programs, there are a number of online affiliate directories. Some directories, such as Associate Programs (www.associateprograms.com), provide links to sites that already take part in schemes and include discussion groups where you can ask questions of affiliate schemes. Other directories include Site Cash (www.sitecash.com) and Net Affiliate (www.netaffiliate.com).

SELLING AD SPACE

Another key driver of online revenue is, of course, Web advertising. Although the effectiveness of online advertising is now in doubt, many companies still believe it is the most effective way of generating awareness of their e-brand.

The most popular form of Web advertising remains the Web banner – an electronic band of text and graphics appearing at the top or bottom of a Web page, containing a link to the advertiser's site. There are also pop-up ads, superstitials (video-based pop-up ads) and sponsorships.

From the perspective of a site user, pop-up ads tend to be the most controversial. After all, these are the ads which interrupt your Web browsing and make Web pages take longer to download. Banners may not be effective, but they are normally inoffensive, providing the ad is for a reputable company.

Sponsorships usually generate more money than other forms of Web advertising because the sponsor tends to be involved at every level of your site, and will expect prominent branding throughout. Given this, along with the fact that sponsorships are often worked out on a yearly basis, it is important to make sure the sponsor is suited to your site. The *Hollis Sponsorship Directory* provides the most comprehensive list of UK sponsors available.

The easiest way to get other Web advertisers on your site is to join an advertising network. In order to register with a network you will need to provide a site overview and specify your target audience, then it is up to advertisers to decide if your site is for them. The network therefore works on your behalf. Once an advertising deal is made you will earn a large percentage of the CPM (cost per thousand impression) rate that the network decides with the advertiser.

Although you will have little control over who can advertise, most networks screen advertising companies to check they are suitable. Double Click (www.doubleclick.com) and Ad Up (www.adup. com) are two of the most well known international advertising networks.

PRICING PRESSURE

One of the main effects the Internet has had on the way people buy products and services is that it has increased the trend for comparison shopping. To help understand the importance of this it is worth taking the example of a high street shop. In the world of bricks and mortar, the shop probably has around two or three competitors within its proximity. On the Internet, the same shop could have thousands of competitors only a few mouse-clicks away.

Your competitors are a mouse-click away

What this means is that if you are selling the same or similar products as your competitors but at a higher price, you are more likely to lose custom on the Web than you would be offline. Furthermore there are a growing number of comparison shopping 'bots' (or robots – the software used by search engines) which aim to find customers the lowest price among all merchants doing business on the Web.

For instance, if an Internet user is looking to buy a computer or printer they can go to a site like ComputerESP.com and be provided with a list of international vendors. Doc Searls, co-author of *The Cluetrain Manifesto*, has looked at a variety of these sites and believes that they are causing online shoppers to make their decisions on price alone. 'Some of the merchant names may be familiar brands,' he says, 'but how much is name recognition worth given that whatever service I may need is going to require the same trip to the post office anyway?'

However, the rise of comparison shopping does not always mean the business offering the cheapest product wins. What it does mean is that you may have to extend the service you offer beyond the specific products themselves.

According to Doc Searls, the way online businesses have managed to avoid competing on price alone is by encouraging informative dialogue and conversation. He cites the examples of Amazon, which famously presents readers' reviews and rankings, and Microsoft, which directs customers seeking technical support to relevant online discussion groups.

UPFRONT PRICING

One of the reasons why 6 out of 10 online shoppers desert their shopping carts before they reach the virtual checkout is because of the hidden costs some companies conceal from their customers until the last minute. These costs typically relate to the delivery of the product or service.

If the nature of your business requires you to charge shipping and postage fees, it is always advisable to follow the BLUF rule – that is, to provide the bottom line up front. It is not enough simply to assume customers will realize that the price next to a product does not include the extra shipping costs. They won't. Furthermore, if you are selling to overseas customers, it is important to detail how much extra the shipping costs are for each country.

CURRENCY CONCERNS

If potential customers are unable to determine the value of the products on offer in the right currency, it is unlikely that they will make a purchase. This problem can be resolved by using an online payment system such as WorldPay, which enables transactions to take place in various currencies without the need to convert sums back into pounds.

Every internationally successful e-commerce site aims to make the payment process as simple as possible for global customers. However, this simplicity must relate to payment method as well as currency conversion. 'In many countries, credit cards are not popular and sometimes not trusted, making e-commerce harder to deploy,' says George Korchinsky, director of Sun Cobalt Server Appliances.

Indeed, in many countries with a high percentage of Web users, such as Japan and Germany, people are averse to making credit card transactions: in Japan, less than 1 per cent of transactions are made via credit card. As well as card facilities, cheques, giros and bank drafts should also be allowed as alternative payment options.

Taxation is another issue to consider. Simply selling goods electronically through a Web site on a server located in the UK to customers in another country will not automatically make you liable to corporation or income tax in that country. But, according to information from the Inland Revenue (www.inlandrevenue.org.uk), if you carry on any other activities in that country you may have a taxable presence there. The IR advises companies to contact the tax authorities in the country to clarify the position. It is also important to remember that exchange differences need to be recognized for tax purposes.

Taxing concerns for e-business

For businesses trading in various international markets, further advice may be required. Taxandlegal.com, an online expert advice system set up by WorldPay, Deloitte and Touche and City law firm Berwin Leighton, provides tailored information on cross-border trade (including trading restrictions) and at the time of writing costs £50 for three months' subscription.

To handle tax and currency issues successfully companies also need to invest in an e-commerce system, such as Intershop (www.intershop.com), that can handle multiple currencies and different sales taxes.

PROFIT POTENTIAL

As the Internet continues to play an ever more important role in business and personal life, the Web's profit-making potential is starting to be realized by companies of all sizes. To make sure you make the most of this potential, it is necessary to explore every option. However, if you expect consumers or businesses to spend money at your site, you need to make sure that they are supported every step of the way. After all, as the Internet is a 'pull' rather than 'push' medium, people's online behaviour is always on their own terms. In other words, if a customer thinks they are getting a bad deal they will not hesitate to take their business elsewhere.

6

Customers

As we have already pointed out, customer retention is as, if not more, important than customer acquisition. Treating customers well and ensuring their online needs are met is the most essential part of any e-strategy.

Although there are a lot of expensive CRM software solutions on the market, technology alone is not the answer. Indeed, many small online operators have managed to perfect the art of managing online customer relations with next to no investment in software whatsoever.

The other important thing to realize is that there is no one single software product which can cover all your e-CRM needs. According to the Gartner Group, as many as 50 different software vendors may be needed to put together a full e-CRM package.

Ultimately, e-CRM is not about software but about meeting effectively the requirements of your customers. This means specifying timeframes for responding to customer enquiries, meeting your fulfilment promises, keeping customers informed of any problems, tailoring your Web content around their reputation, and on the broadest level, engaging in an ongoing and mutually beneficial, conversation.

TRUST ME, I'M A DOT.COM

Winning over e-shopping virgins

Becoming an e-commerce success is about more than attracting a large amount of visitors. Perhaps unsurprisingly, the hardest task e-commerce sites face is winning over first-time e-shoppers. When asked about building trust, online retailers always mention the importance of the first sale. Harry Ganz from the UK's largest online pharmacy, Garden (www.garden.co.uk) claims, 'the hardest order is the first order: give good service on that first order and you have a customer for life.' Jim McFarlane from PetPlanet.co.uk supports this view: 'the issue is assuring first-time customers that we can be trusted. Once we deliver the first order without error or complication, the customer relaxes and starts to trust us.'

HOW TO DESTROY INTERNET INHIBITIONS

Here are some of the tried and tested ways to rid customers of their Internet inhibitions.

Familiarity

Many e-business experts emphasize the need for e-commerce sites to be injected with a sense of familiarity and references to the 'real-world' shopping experience. 'On the Internet, familiarity doesn't breed contempt' says Sophie Burke of Shoeworld.co.uk, 'it builds brand loyalty. With the use of recognizable icons, browsers are easily transposed from a traditional shopping experience to one that is online.' That's why most e-commerce sites have adopted the shopping basket analogy so that visitors can wander the online aisles, pick up what they want and then head for the checkout.

Endorsement

Your site visitors will probably be at different stages of Internet enlightenment. Some will already know that shopping online is safer than buying dinner in a restaurant, while many others will be very wary about giving out personal information and will need lots of assurance.

Obviously it would be easy to tell people how trustworthy you are, but you will need to make any assurances credible. The best way to do this is to sign up to one of the growing number of online re-assurance schemes intended to calm nervous buyers. A good example is the Which? Webtrader Scheme (www.which.net/webtrader). To qualify as a member, an e-commerce site must confirm that its shopping facilities are secure. If a customer gets ripped off, it will reimburse the first £50 of their loss, with the rest being covered by the credit card company. Any company which fails to deliver on its promises gets turfed out automatically. Other reassuring logos which can build customer trust include those of the Truste Scheme (www.truste.com) and the Clicksure Certified Merchant (www.click sure.com). By getting in touch with these sites and participating in their programs, you can assure your visitors that you're complying with certain Internet standards.

Virtual customer assistants

Virtual assistants are popping up all over the Internet at sites such as www.eye-trek.com and www.kmpinternet.com. Virtual assistants are based around natural language interpretation and are complex to produce. However, there is software that can be used to build your own virtual customer assistant. Kiwilogic (www.kiwilogic.com) offers a 'Lingubot Creator' program which helps you create an assistant that can answer your customer's basic questions. However, advanced knowledge of programming would be required if you wanted an assistant to be more complex.

Virtual assistants can be used in many different customer service scenarios, including:

- replacing a FAQ page;
- promoting special offers at certain times;
- supporting customers after purchases have been made.

The human touch

The Web is often seen as inhuman and lacking the level of personal service found in real-world shops and businesses. People trust each other, not machines. As Yooni Suh, New Media Manager for

Boxfresh (www.boxfresh.co.uk) advises 'start with the basic human emotions involved in friendship and the rest will follow.'

Good communication clearly helps businesses online to keep things on a human level. This is why effective e-commerce sites aim to confirm customer orders within minutes. If customers are kept in the dark about what is happening they are unlikely to feel one hundred per cent confident that what they have ordered will arrive on time and in the right condition.

Confirming customer orders within minutes

The Gentleman's Shop

www.gentlemans-shop.co.uk

The Berkshire Barber, The Gentleman's Shop, established in 1997, used to sell toiletries to only local customers but when the company moved to larger premises it expanded its range and found several tourists, mainly Americans, were very interested in its top-of-the-range grooming accessories (shaving brushes are on sale for £240) and often enquired about its Web site.

The Gentleman's Shop Web site was therefore created in 2000. Although customers buy remotely the personal touch has not disappeared, in fact it has become more important to the company. The Web site is 100 per cent successful in turning problems with orders around because of its unique way of handling customer service. Every order goes out with a hand-written compliment slip signed by the person who packed the box. If the wrong consignment is despatched, the most senior person available personally contacts the customer by telephone, apologizes and sets out the course of action he or she will take to rectify the situation. The same person is then responsible for seeing these actions through and contacts the customer at a later date to check that the customer is satisfied.

The Gentleman's Shop Web site now accounts for 40 per cent of the company's turnover and it can even see a time when the physical shop is mainly a showcase and all serious transactions are done over the Internet.

Tailoring content

Understanding the expectations of your target market and delivering what is important to that group in a customizable way is fundamental to e-business. This is perhaps most evident with the example of a supermarket site, which will be visited by some people who want in-depth information and others who just want to order online as quickly and as painlessly as possible.

Many of the larger sites, keen to focus on what marketing analysts refer to as 'audiences of one', concentrate on personalizing the key area of e-commerce – the point of sale. For instance, Asda (www.asda.co.uk) has spent a lot in terms of infrastructure costs to personalize the ordering process for its online customers. Amazon famously keep a record of each customer's past purchases in order to suggest similar titles they may be interested in.

'There are many ways to tailor the content of a commercial site,' says RedWeb designer Phil Collins. 'Starting with the very basic methods of displaying a customer's name – "Welcome back Mr Collins" – or informally – "Welcome back Phil" – both giving the customer an electronic welcome mat as [he or she] steps through the Web site's door.'

From there, companies and designers can add more complex and meaningful personalization features. For instance, credit card company Accucard (www.accucard.co.uk) has managed to extend personalization right to the product level. The new Accucard site allows customers to design their own credit card based on the parameters of payment, statement delivery options, cash back, interest rate and even the way the card looks. According to Dave Wallace, chief new media officer for Entranet (the e-commerce service provider which helped build the Accucard site), 'this form of dynamic personalization is not suited to the phone or other offline methods. It's of real value to the customer and e-commerce channels are the obvious means to deliver its advantages.'

Clearly the e-commerce infrastructure required to create this sophisticated level of customization is not available to everyone. But even so, there are ways in which even the smallest sites can tailor content to each user's requirements.

Reaching audiences of one

One of the methods used by many information-based sites is to syndicate content from external sources, such as Moreover.com. This helps to provide low budget sites with a continual stream of customizable content.

However, for sites targeting a niche market to start off with, the issue of tailoring Web pages to specific users is slightly different. This is because the product information at a site such as The Whisky Shop (www.whiskyshop.com) will be equally relevant to each user. As Daniel Squirrel, the CEO of eMagazineshop.com, explains 'personalizing content can be very difficult. All content must be very specific to what you are selling. If you expect people to buy online, they need to know every detail about the product.'

That said, even small niche sites often need to tailor their product range in different ways (The Whisky Shop therefore concentrates solely on the quality of its product for its UK customers, while on its US site, at www.whiskyshopusa.com, it focuses as much on evocative Highland imagery). And for sites seeking to make sure the content at one site can be adjusted to the needs of multiple audiences, there are software challenges.

Figure 6.1   Accucard offers a personalized credit card to its customers

'From a technical perspective, it's a case of separating content from context and layout – which is where the intelligent application of XML comes into play,' says M-Corp's Jeremy Hamilton. 'Integrating XML with content databases, as the foundation for your Web site, enables you to change the context of the information presented, and its design style, without duplicating source material.'

It is also worth remembering that the Internet is essentially a *narrowcast* medium, as opposed to broadcast mediums such as TV and radio. In other words, simply by visiting a Web site, users are tailoring information. The way that people move around a site is unique to them, and the more pages there are, the more individual each user's 'click-stream' becomes.

Tailoring information

The F Plan

Although fulfilment – the process of collecting orders, warehousing, sorting and delivering goods, and physically dealing with customers – is the key to e-commerce success, many businesses are found to be poorly lacking.

When the Trading Standards Institute decided to evaluate fulfilment failings, its experience of ordering goods from 102 British Web sites found that 38 per cent of orders arrived late and, rather disconcertingly, 17 per cent did not arrive at all. This survey highlights one important fact: the best designed e-commerce site in the world is useless if customers are put off by poor service.

The problem facing many businesses with an e-commerce site is that people who buy in a hurry often expect the goods to be delivered in a hurry too. This is easy for downloadable products such as music and software, but with physical goods distribution is always a bit more difficult.

It has also proved to be an area where bricks-and-mortar companies often have the edge. Tesco, for instance, has been able to save costs by delivering products from its real-world stores. The main issue though, and one the Web designer can play a key part in, is trust. Clear returns policy information and realistic delivery times (such as Amazon's 'normally ships in 2–3 days') are essential. If a site offers '24-hour delivery', the product will be expected on the customer's doorstep within 24 hours *from when the order was placed*. It is also important to make sure that shipping charges are included clearly within the main product information. If a company offers free shipping on orders over a certain value they need to make it known whether or not that value includes VAT.

Keeping promises

Another factor Web designers should make sure their client understands relates to selling overseas, as exporting brings with it a new set of logistic challenges. The company will need to ask themselves who is responsible for any duty or taxes on the goods.

Most e-commerce sites depend on regular postal services to deliver products ordered online, but increasing competition for customer business is pressuring them to find more complete solutions to ensure the timely delivery of goods. Forrester Research recently advised online vendors to adopt an outsourced logistics solution once their shipment volumes topped 1,000 a day. This is apparently the point at which the complexities of stock management and order processing begin consuming an inordinate amount of resources in small online retailers, who can better manage their delivery costs by outsourcing complex supply-chain management.

Buy Wine Online

www.buywineonline.co.uk

BuyWineOnline was launched in August 2000 and is the e-business arm of Rodney Densom Wines which sells 400 low cost quality wines from around the world. Around 1,000 people visit the site each month and 30 per cent of sales are made via the Web. The majority of orders are UK-based but there have been orders from as far afield as Australia and The Cayman Islands.

The owner of the company, Peter Bowman, believes the secret to a successful Web operation is fulfilment. He states, 'Delivery is everything. If your courier lets you down it can spoil all the hard work it takes to get customers to order from you.' And of course, this is the part that's in the hands of a third party. From experience he has found that using a cheaper company is a false economy when things go wrong, so going upmarket and picking a reliable courier that has an efficient online tracking system is key. BuyWineOnline promises a five-day delivery service, but 80 per cent of orders are delivered next day.

Even when things go wrong, there are ways to salvage the situation. As Bowman explains, 'One time the goods were despatched but the parcel got lost in the system. We gave a refund thinking that it would not arrive but it did, the day after the refund was given. We told the customer to keep the wine as a gesture of good will as it had not been delivered on time.'

Just having access to an online tracking system can help such situations by allowing the vendor to stay on top of the situation. Buy Wine Online has now introduced the Collectpoint service as a delivery option. Customers can opt to pay an additional £2 on the standard delivery charge to have their order delivered to a Collectpoint local to them or the recipient's address. As Bowman comments, 'This will hopefully alleviate the problem of customers not being in when our courier tries to deliver.'

International fulfilment

However, for e-commerce companies trading physical goods, especially perishable or weighty products, across long distances or national borders there are various issues to consider. According to Ion Global's Suzanne Alexander, companies need to weigh up whether it is more profitable 'To either have a subsidiary/partner in the given country or take full responsibility for delivery/fulfilment from home.'

Obviously e-commerce companies with a physical presence as well as a virtual one in their target countries have an advantage when it comes to fulfilment. For this reason, The Whisky Shop recently set up a base in San Francisco to deliver orders to customers accessing its US site.

For companies distributing products from the UK to the United States or mainland Europe the extra postage costs involved can prove a handicap. Michael Smith, CEO of Firebox.com, says of his company, 'Only about 5 per cent of orders currently come from overseas because of the very high postage costs. But we don't want to turn away foreign customers and so try and make the site as accessible as possible for them.' Firebox.com also makes it clear how long a product will take to get to specific countries on their product page and are upfront with the postage costs.

For other e-commerce companies, particularly those with unique or niche products on offer, the delivery costs may not be such a deterrent. Whatever the product happens to be, however, customer support is important. Efficient returns policies and complaints procedures are as (if not more) essential for international markets as they are for domestic ones. Furthermore, if you offer live customer support, it will be necessary to offer this service at appropriate hours to each national audience, not just for the UK market.

Ultimately, international success is a question of matching what you have to offer to the unique requirements of each global market you target. It is important to remember that the principles of successful e-commerce remain intact. After all, efficient customer support, user-friendly navigation, relevant product information, straightforward order details and reliable delivery will be valued wherever your visitors are based.

Avoiding usability headaches

One of the easiest ways to lose potential customers is to give them a headache by the time they leave your site. In order to ensure that your site provides a headache-free environment for customers, it is essential to test it in advance.

Curing customer headaches

Owing to the number of usability nightmares experienced by many doomed Web sites, the need to test each e-commerce site with relevant end users is now widely recognized. The significance of usability testing is also evidenced by various success stories. For instance, the BBC's beeb.com conducted usability tests during the redesign of a number of its key micro-sites. The results were unanimously positive. The Holiday site witnessed an improvement of 110 per cent to page impressions. Furthermore, the *Top of the Pops* site, redesigned at the same time, increased its number of click-throughs to e-commerce partners such as Amazon, Bol.com, and WHSmith by 1,400 per cent in just one month.

As M-Corp's Jeremy Hamilton advises 'it is important to always test, review and "course-correct" all Web environments pre- and post-launch.' This view is backed up by Mark Coombes, the London head of creative for Web design agency Agency.com. 'Usability testing should occur on all e-commerce Web sites.'

However, he also stresses that usability research (of which testing is only a part), needs to be conducted on a number of levels. The actual 'test', says Coombes, 'is really the final part, the validation that what you have created can actually be used.'

Even so, target customers should be brought on board in the early stages. This is often an easier task for companies which are planning to overhaul an existing site. In such cases, feedback can be sought via the site itself, with a page set aside to ask people what improvements they feel could be made. This is exactly what Medisave decided to do before redesigning its site. As Medisave's Graham Wright explains, 'customers did give us the feedback (on the old site) stating it was hard to navigate, difficult to find our contact telephone details – we took these [comments] on board, revamped the design and as a result increased orders by six-fold from the same number of visitors.'

There are, however, other options. For instance, e-commerce developers Entranet use a 'Web clinic' approach to test out concepts and working proto-types with end users, as well as an ongoing programme of evaluation for all their customer sites.

There is also the possibility, at least for larger companies, of using a research firm. For instance, when computer games portal Gameplay decided to assess their Web site design, they used BMRB Direct

and Research International. BMRB Direct subsequently outlined areas for improvement based on shoppers' real experiences of the site.

Even without large budgets it is often possible to assemble a sample group of customers prior to launch in order to test out areas such as navigation, ease of use and speed of transaction. Put simply, the more people who trial the site and provide useful and constructive feedback, the better.

Big budgets aren't everything

This is because, more than in any other area of Web site design, e-commerce Web sites require what marketeers like to refer to as an 'outside in' perspective. That is to say, it doesn't matter how fantastic the designer or client believes the site to be, the proof is in the testing.

'The customer really is king,' says Agency.com's Andy Hobsbawm. 'Consider the customer as the single most important organizing principle behind the business, and concentrate your e-business efforts on giving the customer[s] what they want, the way they want it.'

7

Promotion

A Web site should be considered the start, not the end of your online marketing activity. Once your site has 'gone live', your next job is to let people know. After all, no-one will pass by your online business in the way they might in the real world. Fortunately, the Internet is the most cost-effective promotional tool that has ever existed. This chapter is intended to introduce you to the main types of online promotion, and also to give you a grasp on how marketing online is fundamentally different to offline methods.

ONLINE ADVERTISING

In the early days of e-commerce, online advertising meant one thing and one thing alone – Web banners.

Even today, with a growing trend for pop-up advertising (ads which interrupt Internet users while Web pages are waiting to load), banners remain by far the most popular form.

The trouble is, there are very mixed reports regarding the effectiveness of banners. Those in favour of banner advertising point to surveys such as that conducted by Andersen Consulting, which concluded that banner ads are generally more effective than print or broadcast ads at winning over first-time customers. But while banners have undoubtedly helped generate awareness for big Web names such as Amazon and Ebay, there is an increasing scepticism as to how much they can do for smaller companies.

Banning banners

As Web banner 'click through' rates keep declining, many companies are choosing to ignore Web advertising altogether. The fact is that by concentrating on other areas, such as search engine positioning, companies can achieve better results at less cost.

Perhaps the most convincing argument against online advertising is that it tends to go against the grain of the Internet itself. As Brent Marshall from San Francisco based e-marketing firm Logic First puts it, 'Internet marketing is about conversation and dialogue whereas advertising is, by its very nature, a monologue. Furthermore, however much money is spent on advertising a company via the Internet, the real picture will always emerge.'

MARKETING VIA SEARCH ENGINES

Unless an Internet user knows your URL (uniform resource locator, or Web site address), the most likely way people will find your site is via one of the major search engines. In order to maximize the chances of people finding your site, you therefore need to make every effort to ensure you are spotted by the major search engines.

Although there are literally thousands of search sites out there, most people use one of the following:

Google (www.google.com – .co.uk);
Yahoo! (www.yahoo.com – .co.uk);
Lycos (www.lycos.com);
AltaVista (www.altavista.com);
Excite (www.excite.com); or
MSN (www.msn.com –.co.uk).

Maximizing your search position

Unfortunately, each search engine indexes sites according to different criteria, so there is no one way to ensure you will be noticed by all of them. However, by following the steps below, you will be able to make your site more search-friendly:

- **Register**. Some search sites such as Yahoo!'s, have registration procedures, enabling you to submit relevant details about your site (normally in the form of keywords and a description).

- **Concentrate on quality**. Engines such as Lycos employ human 'site judges' who judge the quality of the top 10 sites in any particular category.

- **Gain links**. The more external links to your site the more likely the Google search engine 'robots' will discover it.

- **Include 'metatags'**. Metatags are instructions buried in a Web site's HTML code, which enable you to include a list of relevant keywords along with a site description.

VIRAL MARKETING

In an attempt to explain the Internet's unique ability to fuel interest in a product or service, Steve Jurveston coined the term 'viral marketing' in 1997. Jurvetson, as one of the venture capitalists who helped to initially finance the free e-mail service Hotmail, had clearly witnessed the power of viral marketing at close range. Within a year of its launch, Hotmail had 10 million registered users.

Furthermore, this unprecedented performance had been achieved with a marketing budget of just US $50,000 (needless to say, this was before Microsoft bought the company). Hotmail's fast-track success has been attributed to the decision that every e-mail sent by a Hotmail user should incorporate the following message: 'Get your free Web based e-mail at Hotmail'. By clicking on this line of text, the recipient would be transported to the Hotmail home page. The very act of sending a Hotmail message therefore constituted an endorsement of the product and so the current customer was selling to future customers just by communicating with them. The recipients of a Hotmail message learnt not only that the product works, but also that their friend is a user.

Jurveston now believes that a viral marketing component must be built into the DNA of every Web site in order for it to succeed. As Seth Godin writes in his e-book, *Unleashing the Idea Virus*, 'with word of mouse you can tell 100 friends, or a thousand friends. Because the numbers are larger and faster than they are offline, the virus grows instead of slows'.

While the most vocal proponents of viral marketing are to be found in the United States, over

Spreading it by word of mouse

the last year many companies in the UK have been successfully adopting viral techniques. Thomas Cook (www.thomascook.com), generated 250,000 new customers through its 'Weekend Breaks' e-mail marketing campaign, while rival travel operator Lastminute.com achieved similar results with their PDA-based campaigns.

Laphroaig

www.laphroaig.com

Smaller companies too, have been using low budget methods of spreading the word. Islay Malt, makers of malt whisky Laphroaig (www.laphroaig.com), used a viral marketing campaign to boost awareness of the brand in the run-up to Christmas. Four different e-Christmas cards were distributed to 7,000 UK members of Friends of Laphroaig. According to the company over 40 per cent of those who received the e-mail (which incorporated a link to the selection of e-cards) went on to send a personalized copy to a friend.

While these examples involve using deliberate direct marketing tactics in order to encourage recipients to pass on a marketing message to others, other companies take a more organic approach. Web sites enabling consumers to engage with each other, clearly have a head start when it comes to generating 'word of mouse' recommendations. This explains why the only dot.com to have received more consumer-to-consumer referrals than Hotmail, is the file-swapping music site Napster. The phenomenal success of FriendsReunited.co.uk also illustrates how 'word of mouse' marketing can work, providing the 'buzz' stems from the site itself. For UK-based gambling site Flutter.com, which has built an online community centred around the concept of person-to-person betting, viral marketing occurs naturally and therefore needs little encouragement. It is therefore advisable for companies to focus on a way to incorporate a consumer-to-consumer aspect within the e-commerce site.

By making it easy for interaction between customers to occur, you will be satisfying the Internet user's primary objective: to interact with other people. As Seth Godin puts it, 'it's imperative to stop marketing *at* people. The idea is to create an environment where consumers will market to each other.'

This view is supported by John Owrid, a management partner at UK direct marketing agency Ogilvy One (which opened a virtual marketing unit last year), 'Traditional marketing strategies have never translated to the Web', he believes. 'As the Net's infrastructure gets stronger, viral marketing gets easier and the rewards for those who can do it properly get bigger'.

The beauty of buzz

Viral marketing therefore completely reverses standard promotional methods such as TV advertising and Web banners where the customer has little say. According to Emanuel Rosen, author of *The Anatomy of Buzz*, 'One of the beautiful things about viral marketing or word of mouth or buzz in general is that all these mechanisms only work when you're talking about a good product'.

However, for companies with confidence in their product viral marketing can undoubtedly prove more effective than Web banners and interruptive forms of advertising. By drawing the customer into the Internet selling process, companies are not only stretching their marketing budgets further, but are also acknowledging the way in which the Internet has radically redefined the notion of marketing itself.

Lomo

www.lomo.com

Daring to be different is definitely a strategy that works when it comes to spreading the word on the Internet. Lomo.com, the Russian camera site which has built a database of photos of people doing 'crazy things', has become a worldwide cult owing to the viral effect.

FIVE STEPS TO VIRAL MARKETING SUCCESS

- **Make a strong offer**. For viral marketing to work, the original offer needs to be a strong one. This often involves giving something away for free. For instance, Virgin Cinemas structured one of their successful viral marketing campaigns around a 20,000 ticket give-away.

  Infecting your customers

- **Make it easy for people to 'infect' each other**. The line of text at the end of every Hotmail message contains simple instructions for getting the service. Also, because the instructions appear automatically, no effort is required to spread the virus. By incorporating the viral elements into the product itself, spreading the word will become an inevitable consequence of using the product (or service).

- **Target key influencers**. Identifying key influencers is essential in any bid to generate word of mouse publicity. Discussion group moderators and e-zine editors tend to have a particularly wide reach.

Figure 7.1 Lomo.com is a viral marketing success

- **Leak information**. Newsworthy information has much more value on the Internet than any well considered marketing message. When Steve Jobs first commissioned the iMac it spread the word (and raised market share) faster than would have been possible via any advertising campaign.

- **Gain permission**. When targeting a database of customers in order to initiate a viral campaign, it is essential that each recipient has 'opted in' to receive any marketing material.

ONLINE PR

While in the 'real world' PR is all too often seen as a secondary supplement to a company's marketing strategy, on the Internet PR is everything.

Offline, a business is always distanced from the media, trying to influence it from the sidelines and hoping for the best. On the Internet, however, a business is a part of, not apart from, the media. As a result, every e-business activity falls under the PR umbrella as everything uploaded onto the Web or sent via e-mail holds the potential to affect PR.

E-PR is, in many ways, more straightforward than PR in the real world. Instead of communicating messages via an intermediary, such as a journalist, information can be presented directly. Having a voice is no longer a problem, the challenge lies in making sure that the voice is heard. The Net is, according to old-school marketing jargon, a 'pull me' medium. In other words Internet users pull information towards them, if it hasn't been asked for it cannot be pushed their way. To succeed at PR on the Internet, it is therefore important to adopt an

E is for everything

'outside in' approach and think from the Net user's perspective.

To do this, it is necessary to acknowledge the seven guidelines outlined below.

Tell the truth

As the democratic nature of the Internet enables anyone to have a voice, the truth is always out there. This means people with a complaint against a company can share their grievance with thousands of others in a consumer discussion group. In severe cases they can even vent their disdain by setting up 'anti-sites' such as Microsucks.com or Britishscareways.co.uk. The more companies try to spin the Web, the more they risk getting tangled in a mess of their own making. Not only do the Web and Usenet discussion groups need to be monitored, but also companies need to incorporate any dissident voices into their own e-activity. Web site forums, message boards, chat rooms and other interactive facilities can aid the inclusion of the audience into the message.

Honesty remains the best policy on the Internet

E-PR isn't about controlling information, it's about conversation. This is a lesson many companies have already started to learn. For instance, when Dunkin Donuts discovered a hostile consumer opinion site at www.dunkindonuts.org they decided to join in the conversation, correcting misinformation as they did so. Instead of ignoring the site Dunkin Donuts actively encouraged its store managers to monitor it and respond to criticism as politely as possible. Allied Domecq, Dunkin Donuts' parent company then decided to buy the site from David Felton (the aggrieved customer who originally set up the anti-site) to use as a consumer feedback mechanism which Felton still presides over.

Inform don't advertise

The Internet enables a company to communicate with all its various audiences be they customers, investors, journalists, competitors, industry pundits or employees. If the audiences want to find the low-down on the company, they will increasingly be making the Internet their first port of call. However, they only want to hear it from the horse's mouth if the horse is speaking their language. Successful e-PR therefore depends on discarding the language of advertising and embracing the word of the Web. The fatuous self-praise which so often permeates company brochures and press releases must therefore be resisted, in favour of comprehensive, unfiltered information.

Involve third parties

The advantage of e-PR over PR is the fact that media coverage doesn't have to depend on third parties. This is also a disadvantage. Without third parties how can the company message be effectively validated? The short answer is it can't. This does not mean it is necessary to shell out for high profile celebrity endorsement. As recent events testify, having the likes of Joanna Lumley or William Shatner endorse a Web site does not automatically result in significantly higher hit counts. What Web users want is, by and large, access to objective information. If the content of a Web site is put together from within the company walls, Net surfers will be able to detect bias. If, on the other hand, unpaid

Third-party politics

third parties are involved, visitors to the site are likely to be considerably less sceptical.

Increase interaction

In the real world people watch TV, read the paper or listen to the radio. These are all relatively passive activities. On the Internet, however, people use information. They are therefore involved with the messages they receive at a much deeper level. While viewers watch a 30-second TV ad they have no direct involvement, but when they spend 10 minutes making their own way through a Web site they interact with and become involved in the message.

As solid and long-lasting relations depend on interaction, the Internet can bring companies closer to their customers (and other audiences) than ever before. The higher the level of interaction, the stronger the relationship. Amazon.com, arguably the world's strongest e-brand, encourages inter-activity at every level, and even incorporates the user's voice into its media in the form of reader's reviews and rankings.

Narrowcast messages

Whereas traditional media broadcasts the same message to a mass audience, the Internet narrow-casts messages to individuals. The Internet's *raison d'être* is choice; using powerful search engine tech-nology Net surfers can pick out exactly the material they want from millions of Web pages. In a world of niche markets and even smaller population segments, the Internet therefore has the potential to become the ultimate communication tool enabling you to target 'audiences of one'.

Whereas for the industrial age choice meant any colour so long as it was black, on the Internet users are presented with a kaleidoscope range of possibilities. When Brand X fails to deliver, Brand Y is always only one click away. After all, if someone is visiting a site from a search engine (and most people do) they are likely to have a list of 10 or so other sites they want to visit.

Learn new tricks

While many e-PR objectives remain the same as those offline, the strategies and tactics involved are completely different. PR professionals have to learn new methods and unlearn many old ones. E-mail, for instance, is an intimate, instant and informal communication tool and as such is not suited to the dry banalities of a press release. Moreover, search engines, discussion groups and interactive newsletters need to be considered as crucial areas on the new PR map.

Don't forget the real world

The Internet does not exist in a vacuum. The identity of a company on the Internet affects its standing offline (and vice versa), just as old and new media feed off each other. With the advent of interactive TV and 'third generation' (3G) mobile phones, the dividing line between cyberspace and the real world is becoming increasingly blurred. Furthermore, as the number of TV channels and magazine titles grows, the offline media is starting to develop some of the characteristics of the Internet. People can now customize the offline, as well as online, media to meet their own requirements. Companies can use both the new and old media to target population groups with ever more precision.

PERMISSION MARKETING

As mentioned numerous times already in this book, your Web site must be at the centre of e-marketing efforts. However, a Web site alone is rarely enough to drive Web traffic your way. Sure, a customer may visit your site when he or she is in the process of buying one of your products, but after the purchase has been made, that person may have very little reason to revisit.

Keeping in touch

In order to make sure customers don't forget about you, it may be necessary to keep in touch. The best, and certainly most cost-effective way to do this is through permission-based e-mail marketing.

When deployed in a responsible way, e-mail can achieve a much better response than more traditional forms of direct marketing (surveys have found that e-mail marketing campaigns can be as much as ten times more likely to generate a response as their direct mail counterparts). Furthermore, owing to the self-documenting nature of the Internet the results of an e-mail campaign can be measured down to the number of recipients who opened the message, clicked through to the Web site, made a transaction or forwarded the message to a friend.

SPAM

The problem is, however, that because e-mail is such a cost-effective marketing tool it has been excessively misused and abused by unscrupulous companies sending out junk or 'spam' messages. Specifically, the term spam now refers to any form of unsolicited commercial e-mail.

Forrester Research predicts that by 2005 the average consumer will be bombarded with over 50 e-mail messages every day. As the number of e-mails arriving in inboxes continues to grow, so too does animosity towards spammers.

E-mail overload

The main reason why spamming should be avoided is simple – it doesn't work. If you are sending e-mail messages to people who haven't opted in to receive them, the messages probably won't even be opened. This might explain why 77 per cent of companies now using e-mail marketing methods only send messages to 'opt in' subscribers according to Forrester Research.

For more information on spam and spamming you can visit The Coalition Against Unsolicited Commercial E-mail (www.cauce.org).

COLLECTING E-MAIL ADDRESSES

In order to conduct a permission-based e-mail campaign, you will need to compile a list of customer e-mail addresses. Of course, in order to avoid being accused of spamming, you need to make it obvious to people giving you their e-mail address how and why it will be used.

Subscribers should also be told how they can unsubscribe. Here's an example of a subscriber message posted on an accountancy Web site:

To subscribe to our fortnightly e-newsletter,
Top Financial Tips,
send an e-mail to list@jonesaccountancy.co.uk
with a blank subject line and the message
'Subscribe Tips'.

To unsubscribe change the message to
'Unsubscribe Tips'.

**Manage your own
e-mailing list**

To make sure as many people sign up as possible, it is important to minimize the information you need and also to give details of the frequency of the newsletter. Many sites (such as WilsonWeb.com) also archive newsletters so visitors can decide whether or not they will find them useful before subscribing. Each e-mail address you then receive can be transferred to a specific e-mail folder and used accordingly. Incidentally, newsletters relating to your area of expertise tend to be more likely to stimulate people, and therefore keep them subscribing, than straight-forward sales material. Within the newsletter you can then include links to other relevant sites and Web pages and even incorporate new content from your site (with a link to your home page).

If you only have a small number of subscribers (say, under 200) it is advisable to manage your own e-mailing list by storing all the e-mail addresses in your e-mail software program. This involves placing an entry within your e-mail 'address book' (all the major e-mail software programs, including Micro-soft's Outlook Express, offer this facility) with the name of the mailing list you want to create (eg 'Newsletter') and then storing all the subscriber addresses in that entry. To send your newsletter to this mailing list, all you will need to do is address the posting to the relevant address book entry.

If, however, your list reaches beyond the 200 subscriber mark the task of managing your own list in this way can become extremely difficult. It may in this case be better to use a mailing list management service. There are services such as eGroups (www.egroups.com) and ListOne (www.listone.com) which will manage your list for free, although you are obliged to display ads at the end of any material you send using these services.

There are also fee-based systems that handle subscription requests and distribute messages automatically. Three of the most popular fee-based programs are Listserve (www.listserve.com), List Proc (www.listproc.net) and Majordomo (www.majordomo.com).

8

Measuring results

One of the many new economy paradoxes is that the Internet is both the best and worst tool yet invented for tracking business results. The main, and most obvious, advantage of the Internet is that it is self-documenting. Every e-mail that is sent, every Web page that is loaded, and every online transaction which is made can be monitored and recorded.

Another reason why the Internet can be effective at measuring results is because of its two-way, interactive nature. This is particularly useful when gauging customer responses to marketing initiatives. As Kevin Roberts, CEO for Saatchi and Saatchi Worldwide puts it 'people open up and share how they feel on the Net – something they just don't do in more classical research formats such as focus groups.' On the Internet, as brand managers and market researchers are starting to discover, people are more likely to give a truthful opinion. In fact, a 2001 Open University psychology study into e-mail showed that people are willing to disclose up to four times as much over the Net. This means e-mail and other applications can help you get a closer understanding of the way your customers think you are performing than ever before.

The major disadvantage relates to the speed with which the Internet evolves. The Internet is often said to move in 'hyper time', travelling at seven times the speed of the real world. A product can move through its entire life cycle in around six months and e-business success is increasingly being attributed to those who have the courage and conviction to think first and, most importantly, think fast. This makes the task of measuring the results of your online activity, an ongoing, and occasionally arduous process. However, owing to the inherent unpredictability of any e-strategy, measuring results at every stage is more important here than almost anywhere else in business.

Working in hyper time

ROI OR RIP

Following the dot.com slump, the three letter acronym most e-businesses are worrying about is ROI (return on investment). Basically, businesses are having to ask themselves: is what I get out worth what I am putting in? After all, if you are investing any money at all into your online activity, you will clearly want to know that the expense is justified.

The only problem with the renewed focus on ROI lies in how exactly you measure that return. Businesses clearly need to apply ROI criteria according to their needs. For example, is the business using its Web site to sell products or services or simply as a promotional vehicle intended to drive sales through the traditional sales channels of the bricks-and-mortar business? Ed Murphy, senior digital strategist at Cambridge Technology Partners, has argued that businesses should ask a few simple questions to help them think about their investments, namely:

- Does the online activity support the existing company, for example, by making it easier to do business with current customers?

- Does it extend the business in some way, perhaps by allowing the company to sell in new markets?

- Does it transform what the company does by taking it into entirely new businesses?

If the main purpose of your Web site is to generate online commercial transactions, then measuring the ROI may be easy. It may even be as simple as measuring the amount of money spent on the Web site against the amount of money the Web site is directly bringing in. However, more often than not, the value of your Web activity may be less tangible.

Measuring intangible value

Anything Left Handed

www.anythinglefthanded.com

Anything Left Handed was set up in 1970 to sell products that were specifically made for the left-handed person. Around 15 years ago the company launched a mail-order catalogue with 40 items and in 1999 opened its e-commerce Web site. The company tests products for sale on the site before it commits itself heavily into buying any stock. As the owner of Anything Left-Handed, Lauren Milson states, 'being a small shop we do not have vast numbers of customers passing through each day and so we can't test market in the same way as a national chain might. The catalogue has a large circulation but is expensive to produce and has a long shelf life so isn't really ideal for test marketing either. But the Web site is excellent for this.' The e-commerce software (Actinic Catalog) used by the site actually facilitates the test marketing process because it is very easy to make changes to the products offered.

The site now sells 200 specialist items and also runs the 'Left-Handers Club'. The site handles 60 per cent of remote orders compared to 40 per cent coming by mail-order. The Left-Handers Club membership grew 300 per cent over Christmas 2001 and the site has also included an affiliate programme.

INTANGIBLE RESULTS

According to international Internet research company Jupiter Media Metrix, over two-thirds (69 per cent) of companies wrongly judge the success of their Internet investments, because they rely too heavily on so-called 'top-line' metrics such as online sales and profits. Moreover, Jupiter discovered that if businesses steer away from focusing solely on the short-term tangible sales and profit figures, to look at the non-transactional benefits of their sites – such as improved payroll productivity and online-influenced sales – bricks-and-mortar businesses find that their Web site's ROI is 65 per cent higher than if they only consider sales that take place on the Web.

'Bricks-and-mortar retailers should not blindly follow the lead of their Internet-based competitors by adopting a laser-like focus on the profitability of their Web sites,' said Ken Cassar, senior analyst at Jupiter Media Metrix, in October 2001. 'A typical bricks-and-mortar retailer's Web site can yield financial benefits well beyond the transactions it generates. We estimate that nearly two-thirds of the total online benefit for businesses will be in offline transactions influenced by online experience.' Indeed, a Jupiter Consumer Survey found that 45 percent of consumers have used a retailer's Web site to research a product before buying it in that same company's store. It also added that multi-channel retailers need to remember that not every visitor comes to their site to make a purchase.

According to this return on investment model, a 'real world' business with a successful e-commerce site is likely to gain nearly two-thirds of its total Web benefit from the non-transactional capabilities of its site – for instance, from customers looking for more product or service information before they go out and make an offline purchase.

'Bricks-and-mortar vendors cannot ignore the impact that their Web sites have on offline purchasing because it is difficult to quantify,' Jupiter's Cassar said. He also added that ROI will be higher for those businesses which understand exactly why customers want to come to their site – which may, of course, be completely different to why the businesses want them to come. 'The vendor that spends its limited Web resources shoring up the transactional elements of its site at the expense of the elements that would send a customer with purchase-intent into its stores may ultimately lose offline market share to smart competitors.'

Jupiter's research supports findings into online consumer behaviour made in an international NPD survey. The survey found that 84 per cent of occasional buyers (those people who say they have made an online purchase only one time or less in the past six months) describe their usual use of the

Internet for shopping as 'I usually shop around online and go offline to purchase.' Incidentally, for companies targeting the youth market ROI issues may be even more complex. This is because teenagers, although they feel very comfortable using the Internet, normally do not have a credit card to close online transactions. Jupiter Media Metrix found that although 89 per cent of teenagers haven't shopped online, 29 per cent research products on the Internet before buying them offline.

THE NEED FOR ACCURACY

The more money you spend on the Web, the more you will need to find an accurate way to measure your ROI. However, according to e-business experts, very few companies have properly measured the impact of their e-business systems, either before, during or after installing them.

The average company spending considerable amounts of money on, for instance, CRM software does not know how to measure its effectiveness. According to research firm Gartner, up until 2002 only 35 per cent of companies planning to install a CRM system as part of their e-strategy will adequately develop the tools they need to evaluate their new system's ROI. Of those, under 20 per cent will use such tools to evaluate the success of the installation over time.

Randy Hancock, senior vice president of strategy at e-strategy consulting firm, Mainspring, claims that 'regardless of industry, people should be asking for more rigorous cases that illustrate both the short-term impact and the long-term benefits of a potential implementation.'

According to John Vallovosi, vice president of US-based copier company Ricoh, 'you have to assess both the opportunities for increased revenue and the minimized costs of new processes in the company. Once you go live, you've got to ascertain the cost savings and make sure the increase in revenue is measured and attributable.'

As we have seen, determining the value of e-business is not about looking at online sales or isolating the benefits of a single application. It is about gauging the Internet's impact on the whole of your business.

A holistic approach

As Peggy Sue Heath, a vice president of Ziff Davis Market Experts, observes, 'harnessing your operations to the Net can critically affect strategy – beyond the improvement of processes and productivity. For example, e-business can fundamentally change the customer experience, a company's products and even its business opportunities.'

North Shore Credit Union

In 2001, US-based North Shore Credit Union made a large financial bet on CRM. The hope was to increase assets, customer loyalty and the productivity of its account managers.

'We are an extremely targeted community provider, and to continue to do that effectively, we have to manage carefully our customer relationships,' said Chris Cutliff, North Shore's CEO. Among North Shore's goals: to generate a digital data profile of every customer within a year, and an even more detailed one for its high-profile customers.

As Elaine McHarg, the former senior vice president of marketing at North Shore and the business owner of the project, explains: 'we needed to attract younger customers who were earlier in the financial life cycle, and we wanted to be able to give them more targeted advice, based on their individual financial profiles. We needed to secure more of the share of those high-profit, high-profile customers. And we needed to manage that across all of our touch points and products.'

The firm was able to leverage its popular online 'financial wellness' check – a Web based data profiling survey – into a tool for collecting more detailed customer data for use by marketing and sales staff. As for the ROI, the CRM project has boosted the productivity of North Shore's customer relationship managers significantly. 'The preliminary numbers show the account revenue from our financial managers is up to 18 per cent after five months,' says Cutliff. 'Our loans have grown 20 per cent on an annualized basis, and our retention rate has gone from 74 per cent to over 90 per cent.'

Using the old way of measuring ROI (concentrating on single applications and online sales), North Shore would have overlooked the majority of the CRM system's potential and real benefits – including the bank's ability to attract an entirely new type of customer. Instead, they would have focused on comparing the costs of implementing and managing the new CRM system with the old way of doing things. The result: the CRM project may not have been funded at all.

ROI YARDSTICKS

The areas companies are now looking at to measure their ROI are varied. Depending on the size, status and overall nature of your business and its e-strategy the yardsticks used could include:

- corporate revenues;
- profits;
- costs and customer relationships;
- business process improvements;
- cycle times and productivity;
- the potential for future growth.

There is an irony in that measuring results often requires further investment in ROI software and metrics such as Gartner's Total Cost Ownership (www.gartner.com) and Mainspring's Strategy

Balanced Scorecard (www.mainspring.com). Other companies providing ROI solutions include Meta Group and Accenture.

PricewaterhouseCoopers E-Business Adviser Real Option Valuation method is another ROI service and is designed to go beyond the tangible near-term results and estimate the value of future business possibilities. The method – which is based on financial techniques – aims primarily to place a value on a company's e-busines activity, and the options it opens up.

'The advantage of all these new methods over the old ones is that they try to capture the often intangible, 'soft' benefits', says Peggy Sue Heath of Ziff Davis. 'Each approach has its limits, but they can all provide insights into the impact of a company's bottom line. Regardless of the method used, the key is to begin with the goal in mind – the desired impact on the company and its revenue and costs.'

ROI AND E-COMMERCE

For smaller companies, expensive ROI solutions are not always realistic or even desirable. Indeed, for some, their online activity is easier to evaluate. After all, the less you spend, the less you have to justify. Small sites, without an e-commerce facility, can be set up for as little as £100 using DIY Web-building software from the likes of Dreamweaver, Adobe and Microsoft.

For sites without an e-commerce facility, the ROI results are often a lot more favourable than for larger companies which have spent thousands on expensive back-end e-commerce systems. For instance, while the massive, US-based furniture site Furniture.com tried to close all its sales online, smaller furniture supplier Thos. Moser Cabinet-makers (www.thosmoser.com) decided to use its site as a purely promotional tool. The only objective for the Thos. Moser site was to get site visitors excited enough about the company to request a printed catalogue.

While Furniture.com managed to generate thousands of online sales, Thos. Moser therefore generated none at all. However, the ROI for Thos. Moser has been far greater. In fact, Furniture.com became one of the largest 'dot.flops' in the United States and went under in 2000. While Thos. Moser is unable to quantify *exactly* how much the Web site – which includes a small interactive tour of how the furniture is made and photos of the cabinets in a home – has boosted offline sales, the company believes it has made a strong impact.

WHAT ARE YOU MEASURING?

For your e-strategy to be successful, you will have to know how you are going to measure this success. Companies are beginning to find their traditional metrics are inappropriate in the new economy. As we have seen, looking at sales figures is not enough. So what else is important? In the early days of e-commerce (way, way back in the late-1990s) the main emphasis was on hit counts. The simplistic logic was that the higher a site's hit count, the more successful it was.

The problem with hit counts

It soon became clear, however that there were a few fundamental flaws with this form of evaluation. For a start, as most people browsing the Web will

Figure 8.1   Thos. Moser uses the Internet as a promotional tool

often click on hundreds of sites before they find the one they are looking for, there can be no guarantee that each hit is relevant. If, for instance, an Internet user is looking for information on the Ministry of Agriculture and unwittingly visits the Web site for London nightclub the Ministry of Sound, the hit will be counted even though it is irrelevant.

'Too many companies see the measuring of ROI as being a simple story of popularity,' warns Anne Engel, a consultant with NetGenesis. 'They count the number of visitors they have to their site. There's a familiar pattern, but the focus on site popularity takes away from the financial side.'

The other, and even more significant, argument against measuring hit counts is that one hit very rarely equals one visitor. This is because a hit is a transfer from a Web server to a Web browser. If a Web page is full of graphics and links, not only will the original click-through be registered, but also multiple hits will be recorded for every single graphic. Consequently, one unique visit may end up generating hundreds of hits as the site visitor journeys around the site. Ultimately, a hit is not an action made by a visitor to a Web site, but an action made by your Web server while the visitor was there. Therefore, while hit counters may be one of the cheapest evaluation tools at your disposal (they can even be downloaded free from various sites), they are also one of the most inaccurate.

ACCESS LOGS

A more accurate, and still cost-effective, Web tracking tool is an access log, which is usually available from your Web hosting company or ISP. Basically, an access log tracks all the activity that takes place at a site. In theory, it should be able to tell you which Web pages prove most popular, how many orders were made, and also how people moved around your site.

The advantage of access logs is that they can provide you with an instant measure of success, whenever you decide to change or shift the direction of your e-strategy. They can also help you work out how long people are staying at your site and (if you have an e-commerce facility) how many visitors become e-shoppers.

Most Web hosting companies are able to send you log details direct to your e-mail account. If they can't you may be given a specified Web address where you can go and access your logs.

The only problem with access logs, and it's rather a big one, is that the data can be incomprehensible in its raw form. The results, listed under headings such as 'reqs' (page requests), 'bytes' and 'host' are often coded sequences of letters, percentages and numbers such as '202–132–0.52% – max72.kctera.net'.

Unless you are a computer whizz-kid, this is likely to be confusing. It is therefore advisable to use a log translation service, which will take the recorded data and translate it into an understandable format. One of the most popular and respected access log translation services is available from WebManage (www.webmanage.com). Similar services are provided by Access Watch (www.accesswatch.com), NetGen/ Net Analysis (www.netgen.com) and WebTrends (www.webtrends.com).

These services can provide detailed analysis of your access logs under headings such as 'Most

Popular Times' (indicating when your Web site is most active), 'Visitor Profile' (providing, where possible, information on where your visitors are based), 'Activity by Hour', 'Activity by day', 'Weekly Stats', and so on.

The prices of these services vary considerably and it is well worth shopping around and tapping into customer opinion via sites such as Ciao.com and Google Groups (groups.google.com) before making your decision. A full list of pay-for log analysis services is located at Mark Welch's highly useful site (www.markwelch.com).

FREE TRACKING SERVICES

The other way to get hard data on how your Web site is being used is to deploy a free tracking service or software product. Although available for free, many of these services are extremely useful and can be tailored to meet the particular needs of your site.

Tracking your success

One of the easiest free tracking products to use is that provided by the UK-based company Extreme Tracking (www.extremetracking.co.uk). Among many other things the downloadable Extreme Tracking software can tell you that most vital piece of visitor information – how people are getting to your site. It is able to tell you whether visitors reached your site via a search engine, another Web site, an e-mail link or by typing in your address into their Web browser. Furthermore, if an Internet user gets to your home page by following a search engine link, the software will let you know what he or she typed into the search box.

Other free tracking services are provided by Hitbox (www.hitbox.com), Site Tracker (www.site-tracker.com) and SuperStats (www.superstats.com).

MEASURING 'SOFT' RESULTS

While sales reports, access logs and tracking services are great at providing hard statistics and percentages, you will also need to try and get to grips with so-called 'soft', or less tangible, information. This is the sort of information that can help you answer the fundamental 'how' questions: How do your customers *feel* about your online activity? How is your e-strategy perceived by the wider world? How strong is your brand identity?

To understand where your e-strategy fits into the wider scheme of things it is important to analyse any media coverage online and offline. Media monitoring services are provided by companies such as eWatch (www.ewatch.co.uk), Durrants (www.durrants.co.uk), Cyber Alert (www.cyberalert.com) and Cyber Check (www.cyber check.com). Online newsgroups and mailing list discussion groups should also be monitored for mentions of your business.

You will also be able to gauge the success or otherwise of your e-strategy by keeping an eye on your e-mail inbox. If you are getting an increased number of e-mail enquiries once your site has been launched or relaunched, this is clearly a positive sign.

On the Internet, there is a considerable overlap between marketing evaluation and customer research. As mentioned elsewhere in this chapter, the Internet is a medium perfectly suited to gathering feedback. By asking key customers for feedback, either via your Web site or e-mail, you will be able to gain a 'horse's mouth' operation of how your e-strategy is progressing.

MEASURING SUCCESS IN ADVANCE

Interaction can also be used to test marketing strategies in advance. Scott Kirsner, a US-based brand consultant who has worked with the likes of UPS claims that, 'there's simply no way that a Web brand can be useful and provide a rewarding experience without regularly asking its audience for feedback'.

This is a lesson learned by two of the largest online bookstores: Amazon and Borders.com. Amazon.com and .co.uk regularly monitors its specialized chat forums, especially after it has proposed a change of strategy.

Borders.com offered its site users the chance to respond to a 'preview' site that launched in May. Scott Wilder, Border's Director of Internet Services claims his company is now 'very focused on how we can listen to the users' concerns and address them in features and functionality'. As Kirsner puts it, 'brand building is no longer a one-way street, it is a two-way highway with traffic moving in both directions. Your customers tell you what they want your business to be and you listen and react. After all, you're in this game to serve them'.

AN ONGOING PROCESS

The 'blank cheque' philosophy of the late-1990s has, fortunately, evaporated, and the word e-strategy is now rarely far away from the mention of ROI in any discussion. It would be a mistake, however, to measure your ROI simply in terms of sales figures.

No more blank cheques

It is also important to remember that evaluating your company's ROI is an ongoing process. It is only by attempting to measure your success at every stage that your e-strategy will be able to evolve in line with the requirements of your target market.

9

Security

The adoption of a robust security system should be one of the main objectives for any Internet trader. A 2001 report from the research company Gartner Group claimed that 50 per cent of small and mid-size companies will be the victims of Internet attacks by 2003. The report also suggested that half of all SMEs that manage their own network security will be targets for Web site hackers and viruses, although more than 60 per cent of the enterprises will be unaware of the attack. But despite this threat, a study by insurance company Clickforcover.com, released in late 2001, indicated that small businesses were ignoring the danger of Internet fraud and e-mail misuse.

The Clickforcover report found that 61 per cent of SMEs said that they did not have a firewall and 76 per cent had no virus protection software installed.

Business under fire

David Walsh, managing director of Clickfor
cover.com, said: 'The complacency of small to
medium-sized businesses towards system-related
risk gives serious cause for alarm. Businesses need
to understand what the Web-related risks actually
are, what steps they need to take to protect their
businesses and why they need to insure themselves
adequately.'

However, Matt Tomlinson, the business development director at security consultancy MIS, believes
that security is a constantly moving target so your
security strategy should be an ongoing project. This
section will show you how to implement defensive
actions to protect your business.

ASSESS THE SITUATION

The main stumbling blocks that businesses come
across when implementing security technology are
the twin problems of complexity and cost. It is very
hard to put a price on your company's security, but
the first step should be to undertake a risk
assessment that examines all of your applications
and infrastructure. This includes day-to-day issues
such as physical access, sign-on procedures and
system management tools.

As Mike Thompson, Director of Research at Butler
Group, has commented: 'It is worth remembering
that attention to detail and fervent pursuance of
established policies provide the solid bedrock for a
successful security system. Organizations have to
understand what the value of their IT possessions
are, what is the commercial worth of their data and
what is the commercial risk in lost confidence if a well

publicized security breach occurs.' Once you have undertaken an e-risk audit you have to decide what kind of security measure you will deploy. However, as Matt Tomlinson from MIS, has said, 'there's no such thing as a standard integrated security system, no one size fits all. No two solutions are ever the same because each customer has different concerns and a different network configuration.'

This problem is highlighted by the fact that there is a confusing array of products on the market and you must ensure that when purchasing more than one that they are able to operate with each other. Therefore, this chapter outlines which security products are perceived to be the best. As technology alone is no defence against cyber crime a company must make security problems an issue for the whole business and not just the IT department.

Beyond the IT department

PAYMENT SYSTEMS

Secure payment is a must, yet many small and start-up e-commerce sites ask visitors to send their name, address and credit card details via e-mail. According to David Creswell, a partner at online shop ComicDomain.co.uk, 'this is like sending your card details on the back of a postcard – anyone at the sorting office can read them – it's completely insecure. E-mail can get lost in transmission, so increasing the risk of misplaced orders.'

Andy Hobsbawn, European chief creative officer from Web design company Agency.com, also suggests offering multiple ways of conducting the transaction: 'If people aren't comfortable submitting credit card details online, make sure there's a number they can call or a form they can print out to fax in, or post with a cheque.' The main providers of security software for administration, authorization and authentication packages are IBM/Tivoli (Secure Way), Baltimore Technologies (Mimesweeper), and Symantec (Ghost). More information on e-commerce software and systems can be found in Chapter 2.

HACKERS AND FIREWALLS

Web site hacking is an increasing problem especially on sites where security issues are neglected. One of the most effective ways of stopping hackers is to use a firewall. In simple terms, a firewall is either a hardware device or software program that protects networked computers from intrusion. It filters inbound and outbound traffic and ensures it meets certain criteria before it is allowed access to the network. Among the most respected firewall software suppliers are Checkpoint Software Technologies (FireWall-1), Network Associates (Gauntlet), and Symantec (Enterprise and Desktop Firewall).

VPNS

If you have a subsidiary office in another location or you want users to access your organization's network from a remote location then you may want to invest in a VPN (virtual private network). A VPN offers a secure 'tunnel' to business partners and customers over the Internet, and they can be implemented simply, as well as relatively cheaply. As Evanna Kearins, a spokeswoman at Baltimore

Technologies, has claimed 'a VPN is one of the easiest applications to show a return on investment.' However, there is a limit to the amount of security a VPN can bring. Paula Palma, vice president and managing director at Entegrity Solutions believes that although, '[VPNs] are very good at letting a specified person into a system... that is the full extent of their capabilities.'

VIRUSES AND WORMS

Viruses and worms are a major security risk to companies with an online presence. Although viruses are often harmless and simply display irritating messages every now and again, they can also destroy files and even reformat your hard disk. Viruses spread more quickly within a densely populated online environment and therefore pose more of a problem for Microsoft Windows PCs than less popular Apple Macs. Viruses can find their way into your system through three entry points, namely e-mail, the Web and floppy disks and CDs.

The virus threat

'Worm' programs can be even more bad news than viruses. This is because, rather than infecting files, they travel over the Internet, usually via e-mail. Once they arrive at your computer they use your resources to spread themselves to other computers, the result being an enormous amount of Internet traffic which leads to crashed e-mail servers and clogged networks.

TOP TIPS FOR VIRUS PROTECTION

The many different types of anti-virus software available on the market are covered later in this chapter. However, there are other guidelines a company should adhere to in order to defend themselves from viruses. They include:

- **Don't use .docs**. If you use Microsoft Word don't accept '.doc' file attachments. Instead, use and accept Rich Text Format (RTF) files. With RTF files the Word text formatting is saved, but they don't contain the macros which spread viruses.

- **Don't use .xls**. Use CSV format instead when using Microsoft Excel.

- **Check security updates for Microsoft**. If you use Microsoft Outlook or Outlook Express, install the latest security updates from the Microsoft Web site.

- **Run virus checks** on files downloaded from the Internet.

- **Back-up your files regularly**. Then if your whole system does crash at least the majority of information will be saved.

- **Use viewers**. Most e-mail applications can be configured to view a received file using a 'viewer'. If an infected file is examined with a viewer, the virus will not infect the environment. Normally a user would double-click on an attachment which would start the application associated with the file type. For example, a .doc file will start Word, an .xls file Excel etc. However, these applications will also execute any macros within the received file, which would enable the virus to infect a computer system.

- **Block the receiving and sending of executable code**. Never open executable e-mail attachments such as .EXE, .VBS, .JS or .WSH. as they can contain viruses.

- **Be careful with spam**. Never open attachments or follow links from unsolicited e-mails.

- **Change the boot-up sequence**. Most PCs are configured so they boot from drive A and only if there is no disk in the drive to boot from drive C. This means that if a user leaves an infected disk in the floppy drive, the PC will become infected. In the BIOS, set the PC to boot from drive C which will eliminate the danger from pure boot sector viruses .

- **Use physically separate PCs for searching the Web**. Not only will this reduce the risk of your systems being infected but will also reduce the amount of time that staff 'surf' the Web.

- **Don't use magazine cover CDs**. Only 3 per cent of all infections are from floppy disks and CDs. However, it is well known that magazine cover CDs have been frequent virus carriers.

HOAX WARNINGS

If you receive a virus warning check it actually exists before you take any action because hoax virus warnings have now become the norm in the online business world. You can find an excellent overview of all the hoaxes and scares that are being paraded at Sophos.com. (www.sophos.com). This Web site also includes a number of articles on viruses, a list of the top 10 viruses that are doing the rounds and sells software to combat them. It will even automatically notify you via e-mail when a new virus warning has been placed on its site. Symantec (www.symantec.com) and F-Secure (www.f-secure.com) also list known hoaxes.

Another good reference site about cyber crime is the Interpol Web site (www.interpol.int). This site offers the expertise of its members in the field of IT crime, and provides advice on IT security and crime prevention methods. It also has private and company checklists for assessing online security and lists all known viruses spread through e-mail.

ANTI-VIRUS SOFTWARE

Software solutions to combat viruses

It is sensible to use anti-virus software in three vulnerable areas, namely the desktop, the Internet gateway and the server. The desktop is the most important area because it is the last place a virus can be caught before it actually infects. Remember to keep all desktops (including laptops) up to date with anti-virus software. Furthermore, although virus software can be updated automatically over the Internet, this is not advisable. It is preferable to use a specialist who can test new updates and software. Anti-virus software is available from Network Associates (McAfee), Symantec (Norton AntiVirus), and Computer Associates (InoculateIT).

PRIVACY

Ever since details from the US Independent Counsel's report about Bill Clinton's sexual activities were published online back in 1998, the Internet

Figure 9.1 The Sophos site includes a wide variety of suggestions on combating viruses

has been inextricably linked to the subject of privacy violation. However, as most Web and e-mail users can attest, the problem is not restricted to world leaders.

Privacy concerns can detract customers from using your Web site and need to be addressed. That said, many companies fail to do so. A report published by Consumers International (2001) stated that the vast majority of European and US Web sites aimed at consumers were failing to comply with international privacy protection standards. According to Consumers International, over two-thirds of the 751 sites studied collect some sort of personal information about their visitors and most asked for details that made it easy to identify and contact individual users. Furthermore, the majority of sites did not allow users to choose if they wanted to be on a site's own mailing list or have their name passed to third parties. This is worrying when you consider that 67 percent of Internet users typically abandon Web sites when they are asked to give personal information (according to a 2001 Statistical Research report). However, 26 percent of people said they would be 'much more likely' to give personal information to a site with a prominent privacy policy.

The reason most Internet users abandon Web sites

When formulating a privacy policy, it is important to realize that the main reasons people are concerned are:

● misuse of credit card information given online;

● selling or sharing of personal information by site owners;

● cookies that track online activity.

LET YOUR CUSTOMERS KNOW

It is not enough for a site simply to be secure, you also need to let people know how safe the shopping/browsing experience actually is. Of course, as more and more people become accustomed to shopping via the Web they are becoming increasingly aware of what to look out for – the closed padlock icon in the bottom corner of the screen, the 'https' prefix and the 'You are about to enter a secure area' notices. But even so, there are many extra measures which should be taken to put site visitors' minds at ease.

Not least among these is a privacy policy, assuring customers that any personal information they give to the site will remain safe and will not be sold to third parties. As Web inventor Tim Berners-Lee has observed, 'the greatest privacy concern for consumers is that, after they ordered enough products, companies will have accumulated enough personal information to harm or take advantage of them.' The privacy policy should therefore be well laid out and easily accessible from the homepage. Good 'how to' examples can be found on the eBay and Yahoo! sites.

Building trust

While privacy policies are important, most site visitors will not, in reality, have time to read them. A lot of the factors which serve to put the customer at ease are therefore psychological. As Andy Hobsbawn, the European chief creative officer for Agency.com explains, 'the Web is a disembodied, virtual space with no human contact to anchor the buying experience and little context compared to the real world. It's therefore incredibly important to make the customer feel comfortable and secure online.'

Clearly signposting security procedures and explaining in plain English what these procedures mean certainly makes sense. So too does third party endorsement from relevant authorities such as Which? WebTrader, VeriSign and TRUSTe.

LEGAL ISSUES

A 2001 survey conducted by Clickforcover.com, an online insurance company, discovered that senior managers were happy to plough money into Internet projects even though they weren't fully aware of many of the legal matters that surround online activities. Of small businesses, 78 per cent said they will increase their spend on Internet technology in the future, but 41 per cent of senior management were unaware of their legal liabilities in relation to both the Internet and e-mail with their business. Because of this fact and also because no system is 100 per cent secure it is necessary to have the right kind of insurance. The legal section of the Business Link site (www.businesslink.org) is a good online source of legal advice for UK businesses.

PLAN FOR THE WORST

If you are unfortunate enough to be a victim of a hacker or virus that has affected some or all of your customers, the worst thing you can do is sit on the information and hope that it doesn't get out. The first step is to inform anyone who may be affected by the breach and, if necessary, the media. The problem lies in the fact that your first response is bound to be that you have renewed the technology and the situation will not happen again. Naturally, the first question people will ask is, 'Why wasn't this technology in place before?' This area therefore has to be handled correctly or you will run the risk of losing customer confidence in your company altogether. (See the PR advice in Chapter 7).

Powergen

www.powergen.com

An IT consultant accessed 7,000 customers' credit card details on the PowerGen Web site by playing around with the URL. When he told Powergen of the situation, the company did not inform its customers immediately, and later even denied the existence of any problem when the IT consultant took the story to the press.

Powergen eventually reported the consultant to the police for hacking but did eventually drop the charges. They even asked him to help them tighten their site's security. They also compensated the customers with £50 each. However, the long-term cost for the company in terms of bad publicity remains uncertain.

Woolworths' crisis management

www.woolies.co.uk

Woolworths, the high street retailer, was forced to close its Web site in 2000 after a security breach. Two customers were alerted by another customer that their details, including credit card details, were available at the site.

A spokesperson for Woolworths said at the time: 'I would like to emphasize that this was only two customers and it was only visible for a short period of time and the two customers quickly cancelled their credit cards. We contacted them first thing on Wednesday morning and have kept them up to speed ever since. They have both been very grateful for the way that we have handled it.'

The site was shut down for two months during which time extensive testing took place, something which perhaps should have been done prior to launch. The aggrieved customers were compensated with an undisclosed amount of money.

INTERNAL THREAT

The enemy within

A report by Digital Research (2001) found that malicious hackers are much less of a threat to companies than disgruntled current and former employees. The research said that 57 per cent of firms say their worst breaches of security occurred when their own users accessed unauthorized information. Another problem was that user accounts remained functioning after the users had left the company concerned. This is a very important area to consider but unfortunately not one that can be easily resolved. However, by adhering to the following guidelines, the risks can, to a certain extent, be minimized:

● Check out job applications thoroughly.
● Only give access to information to those who need it.
● Cancel an employee's account when he or she leaves the company.

Another important security issue is the physical theft of IT-related property from business premises, and yet again this is often overlooked by SMEs. Here are some tips on securing your hardware and software:

● Install a physical prevention device available from all good suppliers.

- If you don't already have one, buy an alarm system.
- Consider security tags.

OUTSOURCING

A lot of SMEs have too little time or money to concentrate on the security of their IT infrastructures and therefore outsource a lot of the security work to specialists. A third-party security solution can save you time but it can bring about another problem, namely disgruntled customers. Customers may be unsure about a third party handling all security matters but this does depend on the size of your company and the nature of your business. The online bank, Egg.com outsources its firewall security to managed security provider Ubizen. The company decided to outsource because Ubizen had more expertise in monitoring network logs and it wouldn't have been cost-effective or realistic to handle such a job in-house.

If you do decide to outsource try and go for well known names and, when you do so, ask to see customer lists. It is also important to check the service agreement thoroughly, assess the staff's knowledge and find out the liability of the company if a break-in or problem occurs.

Another related area which is suitable for outsourcing is security testing. Companies such as NTA (www.nta.com) offer regular independent testing reports which demonstrate due care in legal or insurance disputes.

10

The future

If one thing dictates the future of e-business, it is technology. As new digital and Internet technologies develop, so too do the future possibilities for business. These technologies and applications may end up altering the way companies promote themselves, communicate with their staff and customers, deal with suppliers, and sell their products or services.

Outlined below is a brief look at some of the more significant technological developments. They have been selected not simply because of their long-term future promise, but also because they are each starting to affect the way people are doing business right now.

SMS

SMS (short messaging services) technology enables mobile phone users to send each other short text messages across mobile networks. 'Having initially appealed as a cheap and handy communication tool for youngsters, it is now being rapidly adopted by the adult community,' says Paul Collins, a senior advisor at management consulting firm and new media specialists, AT Kearney.

Certain businesses have already started to recognize this technological trend. For instance, Channel Four in the UK and Deutsche Bank in Germany have both used SMS as a means of targeting customers. According to Torsten Barnitzke, head of e-commerce at Deutsche Bank subsidiary DWS, 'the meteoric rise of text messaging has opened up a new channel for us to communicate with our clients. The move also demonstrates how mobile phone culture has extended beyond the traditional teenage market – the average DWS customer is over 50.' So while text messaging in the UK is still a predominantly youth phenomenon, it could soon have a wider significance. Indeed, owing to a potential new wave of mass market text message campaigns, the UK's Mobile Marketing Association has put together a code of conduct for SMS marketeers to follow in order to avoid the problem of 'junk SMS' or 'text spam'.

VOICE PORTALS

In simple terms, a voice portal uses speech recognition to interpret the spoken word. In addition, a voice portal can send information from a Web site back to your phone, be it a fixed line or a mobile device. The idea is that you navigate your way to the data you want through answer-machine voice prompts. The portal then brings up relevant information using pre-recorded audio or a machine-generated voice. Once you've listened to the message, you are given the choice of charging up or using another service.

These portal services – which provide information on news, stock quotes, shopping and so on – have been running in the United States for some time and are starting to appear in Europe. In America most voice portal application vendors tailor their offerings for businesses, enabling their client's customers to offer a wide range of phone services (a bank for instance, could offer telephone banking, bill payment and a branch locating service). For large companies voice portals can also aid internal systems and employee relations. Many companies are using voice portals in place of having phone operators. But it still looks unlikely that voice portals will be able to replace call centres, owing to the inherent *slowness* of voice portal technology. However, with companies such as AOL launching their own voice portal ('AOL by phone'), as well as information providers such as Yahoo!, Lycos and Excite also getting in on the act, voice portals look set to be around for some time. The Kesley Group has predicted that the voice portal market will reach US $12.3 billion by 2005.

Talking technology

P2P

P2P (peer-to-peer) networks, which enable users to share, search for and exchange data directly with each other, have been put forward by many senior commentators as the most radical prospect facing the future of e-commerce. Advocates believe that because P2P networking eliminates the need for centralized servers it can offer businesses an increased ability to find and then link up with other relevant organizations.

Having conducted extensive research in this area Andrew B. Whinston, the director of the Center for Research in Electronic Commerce at the University of Texas, believes that P2P networks have a natural advantage for intracompany information and knowledge management. In his view 'a business-to-business community based on peer-to-peer systems combines the best aspects of the Internet economy – a cohesive, effective network of interested parties consisting of file-swapping businesses searching for suppliers, products, employees, or market intelligence.'

Indeed, the potential benefits of P2P networks over centralized models are easy to identify. Decentralized networks can not only be set up quickly but they also enable businesses to refine targeted search and response rates, and allow the spontaneous formation of cross-business communities.

According to Soon-Yong Choi, author of *The Internet Economy: Technology and Practice* (Smart Econ, 2000), the P2P model enables businesses to 'search for suppliers and parts, disseminate information about new projects and products, complete transactions among partners, and share information and tasks to improve customer service'.

The problem the P2P advocates have had to face is that while the benefits are clear, the whole issue of

P2P networking has been tied up with the issues of copyright theft (particularly in relation to Napster and other music file-swapping services) and privacy concerns.

However, the fact that P2P networks can screen membership means that most privacy fears can be eradicated. Likewise, in terms of copyright, P2P software poses no legal threat when it is used for trading content and products created by the members of the network and exchanged with permission.

As US Internet guru Esther Dyson claims 'the real value of P2P will be in handling and validating exceptional transactions between companies'. Already in the technology sector companies such as IBM, Microsoft and Oracle are endorsing the development of a new programming language, called DSML (directory service mark-up language) which will enable companies to take full advantage of peer-to-peer information sharing.

Validating exceptional transactions

According to interactive technology expert David Kirkpatrick, P2P takes the capabilities of the Internet to a whole new level. 'Now a vast universe beyond the Web suddenly appears within our reach. Not only can big, Web-designated servers be searched, but every bit of digitized datum everywhere will be fair game'.

While an effective solution may yet be some way off, advances are being made toward improving navigation within P2P networks. Autonomy, the British software company, has already developed a navigation system designed around the P2P model: rather than relying on keywords, it analyses data for key concepts. According to Autonomy's chief executive, Michael Lynch, 'it shouldn't matter where the data comes from and it shouldn't matter what format it's in'. Although such software can help users prioritize information within a network, it is worth bearing in mind that it cannot yet discriminate between what data users want to put on the network and that which they would prefer to keep from public view.

Another trouble spot which has been identified is that of 'free riding'. A recent Xerox PARC report on the decentralized Gnutella P2P network found that a few individuals provide the bulk of the files that other non-contributing members can then download. By sampling messages on the Gnutella network over a 24-hour period, the researchers established that almost 70 per cent of Gnutella users share no files and that nearly 50 per cent of all responses are returned by the top 1 per cent of sharing hosts. The report concluded that 'free riding leads to degradation of the system performance and adds vulnerability to a peer-to-peer network. If this trend continues copyright issues might become moot compared to the possible collapse of such systems'.

However, it is important to note that while Gnutella is in many ways the archetypal example of a decentralized network, it is not a B2B model (although it has set up a separate B2B network, as mentioned below). With B2B markets, the problem of free-loading is less of an issue because business products and information are always paid for. As Soon-Yong Choi has pointed out, 'there can be no free riders as long as exchanged content is owned and priced'.

In a P2P market, the middleman is cut out of the picture altogether so intermediary transaction costs no longer exist. It also affords organizations greater control, as individual firms can decide which information and products they will exchange. Furthermore, since access to P2P marketplaces can be virtually cost-free it is likely that more organizations will get involved.

Commentators believe that business-to-business auctions in particular could benefit from the P2P model. Updates on items offered for sale would be instantaneous, data integrity would improve, and the overall auction shopping and buying experiences could be vastly enhanced.

While the benefits and challenges have already been acknowledged it remains unclear when P2P will be widely implemented. The real answer to how soon we can expect to see P2P widely adopted is when the standards are ready. For the systems to work, participants would need to operate in unison. Already in the technology sector companies such as IBM, Microsoft and Oracle are endorsing the development of new programming standards based on extensible mark-up language which will enable companies to take full advantage of P2P information sharing.

XML

XML, standing for extensible mark-up language, is a versatile programming language for exchanging data on the Web. An XML document, like an HTML document (HTML is at present the most widely used Web-building code), contains data along with special instructions indicating what the data means. Used in conjunction with other codes, it can then present this information onto the Web.

XML is gaining popularity among Web designers, many of whom see it as a more intelligent alternative to HTML. For instance, XML allows computers to check that developers haven't made obvious mistakes on a Web page such as putting a numbered list in the wrong order.

Ultimately, the key to XML is its extensible nature. It gives Web designers more flexibility and has the potential to create more dynamic Web sites than the comparatively limited HTML code.

3G

Mobile: the next generation

Third generation (3G) mobile technology looks set to bring fast, always-on Internet access via mobile phones. 3G uses Internet protocol which basically means that mobile devices will connect to any online data source in the world. It is an indication of the hopes being pinned on 3G that new media analysts believe wireless consoles will become the main point of access to the Internet in 2004.

For e-businesses the effects of 3G could be massive, as it is expected to make shopping on phones a fast, simple and convenient experience. In future, so the analysts like to tell us, our 3G enabled fridges will be able to tell us when we've run out of certain foods, wherever we are. The fridge will then, in theory, be able to prepare an order to be delivered to the supermarket, which we will be able to confirm.

However, whether this present science fiction will be converted into future science fact remains to be seen.

INFORMATION PRODUCTS

Many analysts of the new economy have already observed that there is a move away from selling tangible (or hard) goods, towards information products. They argue that even where physical goods are sold on the Web, they need to be presented as part of an 'information package'. For instance, Amazon is about much more than selling books or CDs at cheap prices. It is about supplying customers with the relevant information in order to make their purchase (customer reviews, editorial reviews, lists of products, what other customers bought in addition to this purchase, sales rankings, etc).

The rise in information products has already started to destabilize the traditional economic view as first articulated by Adam Smith, that with a small supply and a big demand, you have a business. In the information economy this rule is now belied by a contrary trend. As the supply of an information product increases, so the theory goes, demand for the product also rises.

The rise in 'information products' complicates the market (from a business perspective) as it replaces the fixed and predictable determinants of a buying decision (price, location, function etc.) with more subjective factors, such as the quality and relevance of the information for each individual user.

BUSINESS WEBS

The term 'business web' or 'b-web' was coined in *Digital Capital: Harnessing the power of business webs* (Harvard Business School Press, 2000), a book by Don Tapscott, David Ticoll and Alex Lowry of e-business strategy consulting firm Digital 4Sight. Web software vendor Bowstreet has also popularized the notion of a b-web and is behind

Businesswebs.com, a directory of Web services. The idea of a business web is founded on exploring the ways businesses of all sizes can interact more efficiently with their suppliers, partners and customers by exploiting the Internet.

Instead of focusing solely on business-to-business e-commerce, the whole concept encompasses many different types of interactions, such as collaborative marketing, customer feedback and product design.

Weaving the business Web

The easiest way to view a business web is as a cluster of businesses coming together over the Internet. While each company retains its identity, the companies function together, creating more wealth than they could ever hope to create individually while inevitably losing a degree of control. The rise in affiliate marketing (pioneered by Amazon and CDNow) is the most obvious indicator of the rise in business webs. However, companies as diverse as MP3.com, Ford and Ikea also exemplify this new trend. As well as affiliate schemes, extranets and other 'information exchanges' exclusive to the Internet can be used to help create business webs.

Clearly, the move towards business webs will not happen overnight, but in an increasingly interconnected business world many believe it will happen. Ed Anuff, co-founder and chief strategy officer for portal vendor Epicentric believes b-webs will require a new mindset, particularly in the attitude a company has towards technology: 'What companies need to do when planning online or e-business initiatives is to think about the different constituencies which affect their business, both internal and external, and look at how to link those together in order to create new efficiencies or new potential sources of revenue.'

Even Steve Ballmer, CEO of Microsoft, has

conceded that 'There's no way we can succeed in isolation'.

However, while many choose to view business webs as a threat, many more are seeing the idea as an opportunity. The new necessity for business partnerships, alliances and affiliations broadens the wealth-making possibilities for those businesses willing to play their part within the network.

As Peter Solvik, senior vice president and chief information officer of Cisco Systems has observed: 'The new economy is about reinventing how business is conducted – in every single job, in every single business. The revolution is still going on, and we have to rethink every single relationship within the company and beyond'.

11

Next steps...

The main focus of this book has been on the key areas to consider when formulating an e-strategy. However, owing to the inevitable limitation of space in a slim volume, this book has not examined in detail the technology and resources which may be involved when putting your e-strategy into action.

The aim of this brief section is to help you consider where you can go for further assistance, once you have gained an understanding of how the Internet can add value to your business.

ONLINE RESOURCES

It is perhaps not surprising that one of the best places to look for further e-business information is on the Internet itself. There are thousands of useful sites offering news and advice on relevant services. Here are some of the best:

ClickZ (www.clickz.com). ClickZ is a site dedicated to all aspects of online marketing and advertising, including e-mail marketing, B2B marketing and compiling databases.

FT.com (www.ft.com). The online version of the *Financial Times* enables you to search through material from not only the *FT*, but also a wide variety of news and business sites including *San Jose Mercury News*, the leading business newspaper for California's Silicon Valley.

Use It (www.useit.com). Use It is the online home of the world renowned Web design and 'usability' expert Jakob Nielsen. This site is packed full of accessible papers and essays looking at his influential approach to Web design, with an emphasis on making Web sites as user-friendly as possible.

Wilson Web (www.wilsonweb.com). Dr Ralph F. Wilson's site is another extremely popular Web site aimed at SMEs with a Web presence. You can search through thousands of articles on Web marketing and e-commerce, as well as subscribe to the twice-monthly e-mail newsletter, *Web Marketing Today*.

Sophos (www.sophos.com). The Sophos site is filled with practical advice on the latest Web viruses and how to deal with them and provides free anti-virus downloads.

Epinions (www.epinions.com). Epinions is the best place to go for objective and up-to-date reviews of the latest software and Web services.

TRAINING AND CONSULTANCY

The advice provided throughout this book has been tried and tested through Matt Haig's work with a wide range of business clients. Matt Haig can be contacted via INSIGHT Marketing and People, an international training and consultancy firm:
INSIGHT Marketing and People Ltd
PO Box 997
Wexham Road
Slough, SL2 5JJ
UK
tel: +44(0) 1753 877750
fax: +44 (0) 1753 877342
e-mail: customer.service@insight-mp.com
Web site: www.insight-mp.com.

FURTHER READING

Cheverton, P (2000) *Key Marketing Skills: A complete action kit of strategies, tools and techniques for marketing success*, Kogan Page, London

Cheverton, P (2002) *If You're So Brilliant... How Come Your Brand Isn't Working Hard Enough? The essential guide to developing your image and your identity*, Kogan Page, London

Haig, M (2000) *E-PR: The essential guide to online public relations*, Kogan Page, London

Haig, M (2001) *E-mail Essentials: How to make the most of e-communication*, Kogan Page, London

Haig, M (2001) *The E-Marketing Handbook: An indispensable guide to marketing your products and services on the Internet*, Kogan Page, London

McDonald, M (2002) *If You're So Brilliant... How Come Your Marketing Plans Aren't Working?*, Kogan Page, London

Glossary

ADSL   Asymmetric digital subscriber line. A high speed, high 'bandwidth' (see below) telephone line.

attachment   A file added to an e-mail to be sent via the e-mail system.

audience   Refers to each individual section of your online public. Each business has various audiences (customers, investors, journalists etc).

B2B   Business-to-business.

B2C   Business-to-consumer.

bandwidth   The capacity of fibre optic cables which carry information. The higher the bandwidth, the faster information will pass through a cable.

banner ad   An online advertisement in the form of a band of text and graphics. Banner ads generally contain a hypertext link to the advertiser's site.

banner views   Refers to the number of times a banner has been viewed.

bookmark   A bookmark is a software tool that automatically loads the page it refers to.

Bps   Bits per second. The speed by which modems are measured.

bricks and clicks   Refers to an integrated offline/online approach.

bricks and mortar   A phrase used to evoke the 'real world'.

broadband   High bandwidth technology which is revolutionizing the way the Internet is used by businesses' and consumers' browser software that allows access to the Internet and World Wide Web. Internet Explorer and Netscape Navigator are the most commonly used browsers.

bulletin board   Software which provides an e-mail database where people can access and leave messages.

B-web   Business web. The term b-web was first coined by the US Internet journalist and consultant Don Tapscott to refer to the Information Age's 'primary business unit, in which groups of firms come together over the Internet. While each company retains its identity, the companies function together, creating more wealth than they could ever hope to create individually.'

C2C   Consumer to consumer.

click through   This refers to the act of clicking on a link to be transported to another site. The phrase is most commonly used in the context of banner advertising.

click through rate (CTR)   The percentage of click throughs to banner views.

clicks and mortar   *See* bricks and clicks.

community   A group of Internet users with a shared interest or concept who interact with each other in newsgroups, mailing-list discussion groups and other online interactive forums.

conversion rate   The percentage of shoppers in an online store who actually make a purchase.

CPA   Cost per action. A pricing model for online advertising based on the number of times an Internet user clicks on a banner ad that is linked to your Web site.

CPM   Cost per thousand impressions. Another pricing model for online advertising (the M stands for the roman numeral for 1,000).

crawler   A type of search engine 'robot'.

cyberspace   Term originally coined in the sci-fi novels of William Burroughs, referring to the online world and its communication networks and evoking its intangible sense of space.

domain name   The officially registered Web site address of your site.

dot.com   The term used to refer to a company based exclusively online.

download   The term used to describe the transfer of a computer file from a server to a PC.

e-business   The catch-all term referring to the business world online. It also signifies an individual online business or company.

e-commerce   Refers to business transactions over the Internet.

e-mail   Electronic mail. A message sent across the Internet, or the act of transferring messages between computers, mobile phones or other communications attached to the Internet.

e-mail system   The collective e-mail software systems which allow you to create, send, receive e-mail messages.

e-media relations   The practice of building relations with editors and journalists via the Internet, especially when they work for the e-media.

e-media release   An online interactive, press release sent via the e-mail system.

filter   Software that can discriminate between types of incoming and ongoing e-mail messages.

flame   A 'heated' and hostile message posted in a newsgroup, usually in response to 'spam', also, the act of posting such a message.

form   A means of collecting data on Web pages, using text boxes, radio buttons and other facilities. Forms are used as a way of making sites more interactive as well as for sales and marketing purposes.

forums   Newsgroups, mailing list discussion groups, chat rooms and other online areas which allow you to read, post and respond to messages.

freeware   Free software programs.

FTP   File Transfer Protocol. This is the standard method of uploading content from your computer to your server.

GIF   Graphic information file. Used on the Internet to display files that contain graphic images.

guerilla marketing   Refers to any extreme or outlandish attempt to generate publicity, either online or offline.

history list   A record of visited Web pages you can access through your browser. It can help you find sites you haven't been able to bookmark.

hits   A hit is a transfer from a server to a browser. Each time a browser transfers a text page that has no graphics, that represents one hit. If the page has a graphic inside it, that's two hits.

home page   The first and or main page on a Web site.

HTML   Hypertext mark-up language. A computer code used to build and develop Web pages.

hypertext links   Generally found on Web pages (although they can be used in e-mail messages), hypertext links link onto HTML pages and documents.

Hypertime   Refers to the fast moving pace of the Internet, as well as the decentralized nature of online time.

information overload   The situation of having so much information on your site as to bore or intimidate your customer.

Internet   The global network of computers accessed with the aid of a modem. The Internet includes Web sites, e-mail, newsgroups, and other forums. This is a public network, though many of the computers connected to it are also part of Intranets. It uses the Internet Protocol (IP) as a communication standard.

Intranet   Internal, private computer networks using Internet technology to allow communication between individuals within organizations.

IRC   Internet relay chat. Provides a way of communicating in real time with people on the Internet.

ISP   Internet service provider. A firm that provides Internet services such as e-mail and Web hosting facilities.

itchy finger syndrome   A slang reference to the Internet users' hunger for interactivity.

java   Web programming language that works on any computing platform.

junk mail   *See* spam.

keywords   Words used by search engines to help find and register sites.

links   Text or graphic icons that move you to different Web pages or sites. Links are activated by clicking them with a mouse.

log on/off   To access/leave the Internet.

lower level domain   The main part of the domain name. For most e-business sites this is usually the company or brand name.

lurk   To read messages in newsgroups or mailing list discussion groups, but not post anything yourself.

mail server   A remote computer (usually your ISP) enabling you to send and receive e-emails.

mailing list   A collection of e-mail addresses.

m-commerce   Mobile commerce. E-commerce via mobile phones using WAP and other technologies.

navigation   The way a visitor travels around, or is directed around a Web site, via links.

Net   Short for Internet.

Net-head   Internet obsessed individual.

Netiquette   The etiquette of the Internet. It is used mainly in the contact of e-mail and newsgroup communication.

newsgroups   Collectively referred to as the 'Usenet', newsgroups are online discussion areas centred around a subject of common interest. People post messages to the groups which all the other members can read. There are over 40,000 active newsgroups on the Internet covering topics as diverse as social welfare reform and South Park.

niche   A narrow but unified market or audience segment. The Internet is particularly suited to niche markets and audiences.

NNTP   Network News Transport Protocol. In newsgroups NNTP is the method by which newsreader software communicates with news servers across the Internet.

offline   Used to denote any activity or situation which does not involve being connected to the Internet.

online   The state of being connected via a modem to the Internet.

operating system   Software stored in a computer which controls hardware components and the processes that run on them.

P2P   Peer-to-peer. Referring to technology which allows Internet users to download compressed files from other users. Can also stand for 'path to profitability' which investors look for in new Internet start-ups.
plaintext   Text that is encoded and contains no layout information, non-HTML text.

rank   A search engine position.
real world   Everything outside the Internet.
refresh   The act of reloading a Web site page or site.
robot   A tool used by search engines to find and examine Web sites.

search engine   A site which enables you to conduct a keyword search of indexed information on its database. Also refers to the software used in this process.
secure server   Hardware and software which secures e-commerce credit card transactions so there is no risk of people gaining access to credit card details online.
snail mail   Net-head term for the 'real world' postal service.
snooze news   Company news which will not interest journalists or editors.
spam   Junk mail on the Internet, normally in the form of unsolicited and unwelcome e-mail messages. The term issued most frequently in the context of newsgroups referring to the same article being posted repeatedly to different newsgroups. The term is a reference to the famous Monthy Python 'spam, spam, spam' sketch where spam is served with everything.

spider   A type of search engine robot.
SSL   Secure sockets layer. The main type of secure server used to take orders online and to transfer sensitive information.

top level domain   The concluding part of a domain name, such as the .com or .co.uk suffixes.
traffic   The number of people visiting your site.

URL   Uniform resource locator. A full Web address, for example: http//www.yac.com

visitors   The people who come to your Web site.

WAP   Wireless Application Protocol. The mobile equivalent of HTML.
Web master   Someone in charge of a Web site.
Web page   A single document stored at a Web site. A single Web browser window displays a single Web page at a time.
Web site   A collection of Web pages.
World Wide Web/Web   The World Wide Web does not mean the Internet. The World Wide Web is, in fact, a software system running across the Internet. It consists of billions of Web pages, usually containing text, images and HTML links.

Index